# THE ESSENTIAL FEDERALIST

# CONSTITUTIONAL HERITAGE SERIES

JOHN P. KAMINSKI AND RICHARD LEFFLER
*General Editors*

FEDERALISTS AND ANTIFEDERALISTS
*The Debate Over the Ratification of the Constitution*

A NECESSARY EVIL?
*Slavery and the Debate Over the Constitution*

THE ESSENTIAL FEDERALIST
*A New Reading of The Federalist Papers*

CONSTITUTIONAL HERITAGE SERIES

*Volume III*

# THE ESSENTIAL FEDERALIST

## *A New Reading of The Federalist Papers*

*Edited by*

QUENTIN P. TAYLOR

*Published for*
*The Center for the Study of the*
*American Constitution*

MADISON HOUSE

*Madison* 1998

Taylor, Ed.
*The Essential Federalist*

Copyright © 1998 by Madison House Publishers, Inc.
All rights reserved.

Printed in the United States of America

LIBRARY OF CONGRESS CATALOGING-IN-PUBLICATION DATA

Federalist.
The essential Federalist : a new reading of the Federalist papers / edited by
Quentin P. Taylor.
  p. cm. — (Constitutional heritage series ; v. 3)
  "Published for the Center for the Study of the American Constitution."
  Includes bibliographical references and index.
  ISBN 0-945612-60-5 (alk. paper). — ISBN 0-945612-61-3 (pbk. : alk. paper)
  1. Constitutional history—United States—Sources. I. Hamilton,
Alexander, 1757–1804. II. Madison, James, 1751–1836. III. Jay, John, 1745–
1829. IV. Taylor, Quentin P., 1964– . V. Title. VI. Series.
KF4515.F38 1998
342.73'029—DC21             98-19391
                             CIP

Volume III in the
CONSTITUTIONAL HERITAGE SERIES
ISSN 0895-9633

Published for
The Center for the Study of the American Constitution
by
MADSION HOUSE PUBLISHERS, INC.
P.O. Box 3100, Madison, Wisconsin 53704

FIRST EDITION

# Contents

*For Thomas E. Baker—*
*A Friend of Publius*

# Foreword

HISTORIANS, LIKE JUDGES, BUILD upon precedent. Once in a great while, a radical new interpretation or an ingenious synthesis of previous writings flashes across the pages of historiography to gain a loyal following. Perhaps only half a dozen such original authorities have broken new ground in the study of the Revolutionary era in American history since Charles A. Beard's *An Economic Interpretation of the Constitution of the United States* was published in 1913.

But for two hundred years, the method for studying *The Federalist Papers*, the greatest American political discourse ever written, has remained unchanged. Ever since the original newspaper publications of the eighty-five essays gave way to the two-volume edition published in 1788, a stream of large one-volume editions has poured forth—not only in English but in several different languages including most recently in Japanese and German. Sometimes excerpts of individual essays or a selection of a handful of the essays were published in a more palatable dosage. Not until 1981 was this publication pattern broken. Instead of a self-standing publication of all the essays (over 550 pages) or some excerpted subset, *The Documentary History of the Ratification of the Constitution* published the full text of the eighty-five essays chronologically amidst all of the other Federalist and Antifederalist publications of the day. For the first time *The Federalist Papers* were integrated into the larger public debate and put into historical context.

Not, however, until the publication of this volume edited by Quentin P. Taylor has a fresh perspective—a new reading—of *The Federalist Papers* occurred. As a student of the humanities, with a special interest in the political classics, Taylor was able to break away from the predictable routine of presenting all eighty-five numbers or a selection of excerpts taken from a few of the essays. Taylor first asked the question "What did the authors of *The Federalist Papers* wish to convey to their readers?" He answered that question with a list of nine chapters, each introduced with a concise, easily understood analytical essay. He then plowed through each of the eighty-five essays and, when appropriate, transferred a portion of the text (sometimes the entire essay) to one of his nine chapters. Each piece of this textual mosaic is clearly marked to indicate its origin. The result is astounding. In 120 pages (less than one-quarter of the original length) Taylor has managed to provide a thorough picture of what Hamilton, Madison, and Jay wanted to convey to their readers. The best of the writing and all of the key ideas have been preserved. Taylor has truly opened the door to this American classic for countless numbers of students and others for whom the unabridged edition is daunting.

Skeptics might criticize this adaptation of the classic, saying it doesn't do justice to the full work or that it changes the meaning. Neither of these criticisms is justified. Rather, for the first time, Taylor has made *The Federalist Papers* truly accessible to everyone. Taylor has pieced together *The Essential Federalist* in much the same fashion that Thomas Jefferson created his own "wee-little book" of the "Philosophy of Jesus" by cutting the words of Jesus verse by verse from the four Gospels and arranging them in "46 pages of pure and unsophisticated doctrines." After reading Taylor's version, anyone interested in the original version can choose from a half dozen editions of the entire series still in print.

If this were all that Dr. Taylor has provided, the contribution would be enormous. But two other parts of this book also deserve notice. First, by weaving together biographical and political history, Taylor has skillfully described the careers of the three writers of *The Federalist Papers* and laid out the history of the American Revolutionary era. Then, in a fascinating essay, he places the writing of *The Federalist Papers* in the context of the Enlightenment that swept across Europe and played itself out in the New World as Americans used the new scientific method to search for effective government that would preserve liberty. Quite simply, Quentin Taylor has brought a breath of fresh air to the study of what had become a rather stuffy discussion among a handful of learned scholars. Taylor's *The Essential Federalist* democratizes the study of this masterpiece of political theory.

JOHN P. KAMINSKI
*Center for the Study of the American Constitution*
*University of Wisconsin–Madison*

# Preface

LIKE THE UNITED STATES Constitution, *The Federalist* is often quoted, but less frequently read. Given its brevity (about twenty pages, including amendments) there can be little excuse for this in the case of America's fundamental law. *The Federalist*, however, is a much lengthier document of some 500 pages. Moreover, the work has no clear divisions—no subject headings or chapter titles—to orient the reader to its contents. The method used to distinguish one "paper" from another is, indeed, the most nondescript of all: numbering. More daunting for some is the language itself; undeniably eloquent, yet dense, occasionally discursive, and slightly archaic. Finally, much contained in *The Federalist* may be described as "lifeless" and of little abiding interest to today's general reader. The papers, after all, were written within a particular context, for a specific purpose, and in an age remote from our own.

In combination, these features of *The Federalist*—a document rivaled in importance only by the Declaration of Independence and the U.S. Constitution—have rendered it less well-known to the American public than might otherwise be the case. What direct exposure does exist typically takes the form of readings from *Federalist* Nos. 10 and 51 in the undergraduate American Government course. As one who has regularly taught this course, I have observed that the initial response to these selections is more often one of bewilderment than understanding. Yet with some assistance, most students can be brought to a fundamental grasp of the authors' central ideas, and in some cases, a genuine appreciation.

I suspect, however, that for many the experience of reading from *The Federalist* is not a particularly pleasant one. And like the proverbial reading of Shakespeare in high school, it often results in an unfortunate consequence: the initial bad taste spoils the appetite for life. This is hardly to suggest that life without Shakespeare or *The Federalist* is not worth living, but rather, that many among the otherwise indifferent might come to explore and appreciate these classics under more favorable conditions. The desire to contribute to this prospect in the case of *The Federalist* accounts for the genesis and final form of this volume.

The key to facilitating an expanded readership for *The Federalist* lies in making the text more accessible. Doing so, however, demands something more than the typical practice of extracting and arranging a series of "representative" selections. Rather, it requires the adoption of a more discriminating approach; viz., one that aims to isolate those portions of the work which continue to inform and instruct, an approach that showcases *The* "essential" *Federalist*.

With this criterion as a guide, the editing process achieves the following: first, it reduces *The Federalist* to approximately one-fifth of its original length; second, it eliminates what is incidental to the text or no longer relevant for today's reader; and third, it permits an arrangement of the living content of each "paper" under appropriate subject headings. (Several of the selections could appear under more than one heading, and in such cases, placement has been determined according to emphasis. This minor inconvenience is, I believe, more than offset by the advantages of topical arrangement.) "The Essential *Federalist*," then, is no mere anthology or abridgement, but a unique compendium drawn from what Thomas Jefferson called "the best commentary on the principles of government which was ever written."

As for difficulties of language and style, there can be no relief. While I have updated spellings and punctuation, I have in no instance modified vocabulary or syntax. Yet as with Shakespeare (who is more challenging in this regard than the authors of *The Federalist*), it will be found that a little effort will go a long way when it comes to "deciphering" troublesome passages.

I am sure there are a few purists who will object to this "cut and paste" approach to *The Federalist*. For these there are some half-dozen unabridged editions of the work currently in print. More to the point, this book was not compiled for purists or specialists, but for students, teachers, and citizens. These, I can assure, may confidently use this text for purposes of instruction, research, and citation: nothing included has been unduly taken out of context, and nothing excluded compromises the integrity of what is contained. The source text for this edition is *The Documentary History of the Ratification of the Constitution*, edited by Merrill Jensen, et al. (Madison, Wis., 1976– ) which reproduces the original versions of the eighty-five *Federalist* papers.

To help the reader "place" *The Federalist* in its proper historical setting, I have chronicled the relevant events of the Founding era via biographical sketches of its authors—Alexander Hamilton, James Madison, and John Jay. In breadth and depth these remarks go well beyond the standard introductions found in current editions of *The Federalist*. Another distinctive feature of the present volume is the inclusion of an interpretive essay in which I examine how the authors' mode of analysis informs their political prescriptions and "reading" of the Constitution. Those interested in the extensive literature on *The Federalist* (and related subjects) should consult the essay's endnotes.

It is my hope that the combined features of this work will foster a greater acquaintance with, understanding of, and appreciation for *The Federalist* and the "miracle" of the American Founding.

I would like to thank Ms. Lori Pennington for her assistance in reviewing the manuscript prior to submission for publication. Thanks also to Mr. William Feeler (Midland College) and Dr. George W. Carey (Georgetown University) for reading drafts of the introduction and essay. I also wish to acknowledge Dr. Richard Leffler (University of Wisconsin-Madison) for his helpful review of the headnotes. Special thanks to Constitutional Heritage Series editor Dr. John P. Kaminski whose assistance in preparing this volume for publication was indispensable.

QUENTIN P. TAYLOR
*Austin, Texas*

*If the road over which you will still have to pass [in reading these papers] should in some places appear to you tedious or irksome, you will recollect that you are in quest of information on a subject the most momentous which can engage the attention of a free people: that the field through which you have to travel is in itself spacious, and that the difficulties of the journey have been unnecessarily increased by the mazes with which sophistry has beset the way. It will be my aim to remove the obstacles to your progress in as compendious a manner as it can be done, without sacrificing utility to dispatch. (No. 15)*

*—Publius*

# Hamilton, Madison, and Jay: An Introduction

T*he Federalist* IS AN EMINENTLY straightforward document. There is nothing ambiguous about its purpose or esoteric about its meaning. This fact owes much to the specific goal to which the work was directed, and to the intellectual and literary brilliance of its authors. In short, there is little that can be said about the *contents* of *The Federalist* that is not better stated by "Publius" himself. Still, it is necessary for the reader to be acquainted with the historical *context* of *The Federalist* in order to better appreciate its meaning and significance. In particular this entails some knowledge of the "critical period" under the Articles of Confederation (1781–1789), the proceedings of the Federal Convention in Philadelphia (1787), and the ratification contest which followed (1787–88). It was during this last period that *The Federalist* was composed: a series of eighty-five essays written to defend the Constitution from its detractors, explain its provisions in detail, and encourage its adoption by the people of New York. Since its inception, the work has been widely recognized as the most authoritative commentary on the Constitution and America's greatest contribution to political thought. A glance at the public lives of the remarkable trio who authored the papers will provide the biographical and historical backdrop required for a more informed reading of "The Essential *Federalist*."

# Alexander Hamilton
# (1757–1804)

THE IDEA FOR *The Federalist* originated with Alexander Hamilton. Born on the island of Nevis in the British West Indies, Hamilton was the illegitimate son of a fallen Scottish aristocrat and a "dissolute" Huguenot mother who died when he was still a boy. Virtually an orphan, Alexander was employed in a commercial firm on St. Croix at the age of eleven. While confessing a contempt for "the grovelling condition of a clerk," he nonetheless displayed such extraordinary poise and maturity, that by thirteen he was running the business. Impressed by his abilities, and sensing his great promise, some admiring neighbors arranged to send the youngster to the mainland colonies for a formal education.

Not long after he arrived in New York in 1773, Hamilton entered King's College (now Columbia), where he distinguished himself as a precocious learner and an assiduous student. In the wake of the "Intolerable Acts" (imposed by Britain in retaliation for the Boston Tea Party), he made his first major foray into politics by writing two pamphlets defending the American cause. The high quality of these writings, all the more remarkable for the youth of their author, catapulted Hamilton into the vanguard of the New York resistance movement.

Following the clashes at Lexington and Concord in April 1775, Hamilton helped form a militia company and saw action when his unit rescued a number of cannon while under bombardment by a British warship. Anticipating a full-scale conflict, he secured a commission as captain of artillery in the spring of 1776. When the British invaded New York, the young officer fought with notable distinction and caught the eye of George Washington, commander-in-chief of the American forces. To Hamilton's disappointment, the General was more interested in his gifted pen than in his budding sword, and asked the young warrior to serve as his personal secretary. Hamilton accepted the offer, was promoted to the rank of lieutenant colonel, and for the next four years (1777–1781) was engrossed in his duties, which included the reorganization of the Continental Army.

While Hamilton's superior talents gained him the complete confidence of Washington, the romantic youth hungered for military glory. Impatient with his sedentary tasks, he provoked a quarrel with the General, resigned as aide-de-camp, and was permitted to return to active

duty in the field. At the decisive Battle of Yorktown (1781), which secured America's independence, Hamilton distinguished himself by leading
a victorious assault on the enemy's fortified position. Some time before
these heroics, the young colonel married Elizabeth Schuyler, the daughter of wealthy patrician General Philip Schuyler. His marriage to "Betsy"
was one of mutual affection, but it also had the advantage of aligning
Hamilton with one of New York's leading families.

After the British surrender at Yorktown, Hamilton retired from the
army, returned to New York, and in 1782 was appointed continental tax
receiver, his first public office. At the same time, he read law and, after a
few months of intensive study, was admitted to practice. Shortly thereafter Hamilton was chosen to represent New York in Congress. Hamilton
recognized sooner than most that the Articles of Confederation, which
had been formally adopted on March 1, 1781, failed to invest the central
government with sufficient authority to govern effectively. Most fatal
was Congress's lack of the taxing power: it could (and did) levy "assessments" on the states, but it had no authority to enforce their payment.
These "requisitions" were never met in full, and at times went unpaid
altogether. Another potential source of income, a duty on imports, was
also denied Congress under the Articles. Amendments authorizing Congress to levy a modest impost (or tariff) gained the support of twelve of
thirteen states on two separate occasions, but failed to gain the unanimous support required under the Articles. Accordingly, the government
was chronically short of revenue and found itself unable to meet its most
basic financial obligations.

Among the unpaid were members of the Continental Army, who
grew increasingly restive following the defeat of the first impost in late
1782. Near the point of desperation, Hamilton and others in Congress
contemplated using unrest in the army to force the issue of financial
reform. While the so-called "Newburgh Conspiracy" was nipped in the
bud, Congress did pass a new revenue bill (subject to the unanimous
approval of the state legislatures) and some of the soldiers were paid.
This was not sufficient, however, to pacify them all, and when elements
of the Pennsylvania militia marched on Philadelphia, Congress decided
to desert the "city of brotherly love."

Disgusted by events, Hamilton resigned from Congress and returned
to New York, where he established a law practice on Wall Street. Some
of his first clients were American loyalists (or Tories) who were sued
under the state's Trespass Act for compensation for the use of patriot-
owned property in British occupied areas. As the measure was highly
popular, Hamilton's attack on its legality was met with a predictable out-
cry. Deeply committed to property rights, and hoping to make friends

out of former enemies, the controversial attorney defended his actions in two letters published under the signature of "Phocian" in 1784. Due in no small part to Hamilton's efforts, the Trespass Act was eventually repealed, and by 1787 the rights of former loyalists were restored in full. During the same period, Hamilton became increasingly interested in financial matters and shortly became an authority on the subject. In 1784 he helped found and became a director of the Bank of New York, a position that anticipated his role as the first secretary of the treasury under the Constitution. The tireless Hamilton even found time to assist in the formation of the New York Abolition Society, an association committed to the gradual abolition of slavery in the Empire State.

Occupied with these matters and with the responsibilities of a growing family, Hamilton contemplated abandoning politics altogether. Ill-suited to remain on the sidelines, he sought and won election to the state assembly in 1786. With a dire sense of urgency, Hamilton embarked on a mission to save the faltering republic. In a renewed battle over the continental impost, he argued forcefully on behalf of the measure, but failed to obtain the legislature's unqualified support. He did, however, succeed in being appointed to represent New York at an interstate commercial convention in Annapolis, Maryland. When delegates from only five states attended, Hamilton persuaded those present to issue a call for a general convention to meet at Philadelphia in May 1787. Only in the context of broad reform, he argued, could the problems of interstate commerce be successfully resolved. In a statement drafted by Hamilton, the Annapolis commissioners called on each state to send delegates to a federal convention in order to devise such provisions "as shall appear to them necessary to render the constitution of the Federal Government adequate to the exigencies of the Union." When the proposal reached Congress and the states, there was little momentum for a constitutional convention. Few nationalists were still sitting in Congress, and state officials tended to view with suspicion plans to strengthen the general government. Not until the climax of Shays' rebellion in February of 1787 did the majority of states, and Congress itself, authorize the meeting. The uprising played into the hands of Hamilton and the nationalists, who used the incident to fan popular fears of class warfare and impending anarchy. The forces for revising America's fundamental law had finally reached a critical mass.

Following the suppression of the Shaysites, Hamilton was selected as one of New York's three delegates to the Federal Convention. Convinced that the Articles of Confederation were beyond repair, he was among those who advocated the creation of a strong national government that would act directly on the people. (Under the Articles the cramped authority of Congress extended only to the states, not to individuals.) Hamilton's influence, however, was blunted by his colleagues from New York, John Lansing, Jr. and Robert Yates, who opposed any plan that went beyond revising the Articles. With each state having one vote, Hamilton's voice was effectively silenced, and he took little part in the early debates.

A more serious liability was rooted in Hamilton's ultranationalist and quasi-monarchical views. As an immigrant he loved his adopted *nation*, but he never felt a personal attachment to any *state*; and as a gentleman of aristocratic temperament, he never developed an appreciation for "the spiritual value of democracy." The nation's experience under the Articles had only confirmed his suspicions of divided sovereignty and kindled his fear of republicanism. Virtually all the delegates in Philadelphia were willing to strengthen the central government at the expense of the states: Hamilton, however, was prepared to abolish the states altogether! In a speech that lasted some five hours, a suddenly uninhibited Hamilton diagnosed the dilemma facing the nation, underscored the futility of half-measures, and then presented a scheme of government so "high-toned" in its particulars, that it was met with stunned silence. The audacious plan envisaged a central government possessed of near-exclusive sovereignty, and empowered to legislate on behalf of the states, which would survive as mere administrative districts of the national authority. Inspired by the "mixed" constitution of Great Britain (a composite of monarchical, oligarchic, and democratic elements), Hamilton's "plan" contained the following provisions: an executive chosen for life, with an absolute veto on national legislation, and with power to appoint state governors (who had a similar veto power over state legislation); an upper house chosen for life on a property basis; a lower chamber chosen on the basis of manhood suffrage; and centralized control of "state" militias. Perhaps most remarkable was the absence of any limits placed on the central government's authority: Hamilton's plan contained no specified grants of power and no bill of rights.

The indirect impact of Hamilton's speech is uncertain, but the hushed response of the delegates signaled an apparent lack of support for his plan, which was tabled without debate. Discouraged by the direction of the proceedings, Hamilton left Philadelphia at the end of June and returned to New York. Never content as a bystander, he returned to Philadelphia in August, attended a few sessions, left again, and then returned in September for the final days of the Convention. During his first absence the delegates passed the so-called "Great Compromise" which settled the deeply divisive question of representation in the national legislature. Bending to necessity, but still committed to a "mixed" system, Hamilton now worked to strengthen various features of the executive and legislative branches. His contention that the people should have a voice in choosing the president facilitated the creation of the electoral college.

After Yates and Lansing left the Convention in mid-July, the Empire State went without representation in Philadelphia. Hamilton's return in August did not change this situation, for the Convention rules required that a state be represented by at least two delegates. He did, however, sign the final document on September 17, which was officially designated the work of eleven state delegations "and Mr. Hamilton." Before he attached his signature to the parchment, a resigned Hamilton reminded his colleagues that "no man's ideas were more remote from the plan than his own were known to be." How ironic that this reluctant signer of the Constitution should become an ardent proponent of its ratification almost as soon as the ink was dry! Yet Hamilton had little choice but to support adoption. The proposed plan of union was certainly marred by flaws, he reasoned, but it was far superior to the utterly worthless Articles.

As soon as the proposed Constitution was made public, it was roundly denounced by those who feared it would result in a tyrannical government ruling on behalf of the rich. Hamilton knew that ratification would be an uphill struggle in New York, where most of the political class (including Governor George Clinton) were hostile to a plan that, among other things, would reduce their own authority. To counter the opposition, Hamilton attacked on several fronts. First, he returned to the inkwell and began a series of "papers" intended to sway opinion in the direction of ratification. Such was the origin of *The Federalist*, the first installment of which appeared in the New York press some six weeks after the signing of the Constitution. The title of the work was an ingenious ploy on Hamilton's part, for it positively identified supporters of the plan as "Federalists" (instead of the pejorative "nationalists"), while its opponents were left with the negative "Antifederalists."

To assist him in the project, Hamilton tapped fellow New Yorker, John Jay, a strong nationalist who had served in various high offices since 1774. Also approached was James Madison, a Virginia nationalist who had been a leading voice at the Federal Convention. Like Hamilton, Madison and Jay were schooled in history, experienced in politics, and shrewd observers of human nature. All three were superb writers. In keeping with accepted practice, the papers were written under a pseudonym. The name chosen was "Publius," in reference to the legendary

Publius Valerius Puplicolo, who established republican government in ancient Rome. The cloak of anonymity was fortuitous, for it allowed Hamilton and Madison (who had signed the Constitution) to speak to the merits of ratification without the charge of special pleading.

After Hamilton's lead-off essay, Jay composed *Federalist* Nos. 2 through 5, then fell seriously ill: he would contribute only one more paper after his recovery. Hamilton wrote twenty-seven of the next thirty-one essays, then turned the project over to Madison, while he attended to his legal practice and personal affairs. Encouraged by the response to "Publius," the two principal authors decided to broaden the scope of the project, and arranged to have the first thirty-six papers published in book form and distributed outside New York. In the meantime, Madison composed a string of twenty-seven essays (Nos. 37–63), and then in March 1788, returned to Virginia to attend the state's ratifying convention. After Jay's final effort (No. 64), Hamilton contributed another thirteen papers, which like the previous essays, first appeared in New York City newspapers. The final eight essays, also the work of Hamilton, initially appeared in May 1788 as part of the second volume of the first edition of *The Federalist*.

By the time the series was completed, eight states had already ratified the Constitution, one short of the number required for adoption. New Hampshire's approval on June 21 put the measure over the top: the United States would have a new government. When Virginia voted for ratification a few days later, New York was the only major state still outside the fold. For a time it looked as though it would remain so, for when the state ratifying convention assembled in Poughkeepsie, Antifederalist delegates, led by Governor George Clinton, held a comfortable majority. The Federalist minority included Hamilton, who feared a no-vote by New York would disrupt, if not doom the embryonic union. As the only delegate who had signed the Constitution, the task of converting members of the opposition to the side of ratification largely fell on his shoulders. In this high stakes game with the odds stacked against him, a determined Hamilton marshaled his resources and entered the fray. In an apparent *volte-face* from his Philadelphia performance, the aristocratic nationalist spoke as a confirmed republican and an ardent friend of the Constitution. At the prior convention, Hamilton had derisively referred to the states as "artificial" bodies incompatible with the national authority; now he pronounced them integral to its functioning. Moreover, he asserted that under the new Constitution the *states* would serve as the principal guardians of the people's liberties. In canvassing these and other arguments, Hamilton made ready use of the sagacious "Publius," so much so that Governor

Clinton ironically asked if he was planning to come out with a new edition!

Hamilton's sudden "conversion" to federalism and democracy would not go unchallenged. Yates and Lansing had been present at Philadelphia when Hamilton questioned the propriety of republican government and impugned the states; now they rose at Poughkeepsie to denounce his inconsistency. In response, Hamilton skillfully disarmed his attackers; but for all his eloquence and passion, he could persuade few "Antis" to support unconditional ratification. With the Convention deadlocked on the floor, a discouraged but indefatigable Hamilton worked to effect a compromise behind the scenes. In some of the earlier ratifying conventions, Federalists gained the support of the Constitution's critics by agreeing to attach proposed amendments to their state's ratification articles. The opposition in New York, however, wanted the option of *withdrawing* from the union if certain amendments were not approved within a given time. Unwilling to countenance conditional adoption (or outright rejection), Hamilton accepted the lesser evil of a call for a second constitutional convention. Gambling that subsequent events (viz., the adoption of a national bill of rights) would stall the drive for a second convention, the condition was formally agreed to, and enough moderates switched sides to secure ratification by the slim margin of 30 to 27. Hamilton, who was ably assisted at Poughkeepsie by Robert R. Livingston and John Jay, was justly credited with the victory.

# *James Madison*
# *(1751–1836)*

HAMILTON'S PRINCIPAL collaborator on *The Federalist* was the eldest child of James Madison, Sr., a wealthy, civic-minded member of the planter elite in Orange County, Virginia. Growing up on the family plantation at Montpelier, James, Jr. was a shy and bookish child who demonstrated an unusual gift for learning. The boy's formal studies were entrusted to the care of capable tutors who instructed James in the various elements of a classical education. After seven years of private instruction, "Jemmy" attended New Jersey (Princeton) College, where he was deeply influenced by "the spirit of liberty and free enquiry" that pervaded the institution. Exempted from much of the freshman curriculum, the diligent youngster compressed three years of study into two, graduating in the Fall of 1771.

After a period of advanced studies, a pale and exhausted Madison returned to Montpelier, fearful that his frail constitution would condemn him to poor health and an early death. Small in stature and physically delicate, Madison was apparently suffering from a nervous disorder, a condition that would periodically plague him for some time to come. Following advice to study less and exercise more, Madison's health improved. For nearly four years, however, he remained undecided as to a professional calling.

Prior to 1773 Madison showed little interest in the political struggle between Britain and the American colonies or in civic matters generally. In that year he began studying constitutional systems, with an emphasis on church-state relations. When a nearby county jailed a handful of Baptist ministers for preaching without a license, he passionately spoke out in defense of religious liberty, a cause he would champion with notable success in coming years. Shortly after the Boston Tea Party, Madison eagerly took up the patriotic cause and was elected to the local committee of safety in late 1774. The committee's responsibilities included enforcing non-importation acts, suppressing hostile opposition, and preparing for armed conflict. Assisting in the execution of these measures, Madison displayed a maturity and zeal that marked him as a future leader. A confirmed patriot, he even trained as a soldier for a time and was commissioned a colonel in the militia. Ill-suited to the rigors of military life, Madison's fighting would be done on the political field as a member of Virginia's revolutionary government, and later as a delegate to the Continental Congress. "From the uncertain, introspective, affectedly grave youth he had been in the year after he graduated from college," a biographer of Madison has written, "he had become a man consumed with a cause. He had henceforth his vocation: he was a nation builder."

As Congress prepared for independence in the spring of 1776, Madison was selected to represent Orange County at a statewide convention in Williamsburg. Within two heady months, the body had authorized its delegates in Congress to call for independence, established a revolutionary government, and adopted a bill of rights and a state constitution. In the company of experienced and capable men, such as Patrick Henry and George Mason, the twenty-five year old Madison maintained a dignified reserve much of the time. Yet in his own quiet and unpretentious way, he earned the respect and admiration of his esteemed colleagues. He also made an important contribution as a member of the committee appointed to draft a "Declaration of Rights," when he persuaded the convention to replace the phrase "fullest toleration" with "free exercise" of religion. This slight change was critical, for it implied that religious freedom was an inalienable right, not a privilege granted by the state.

Madison's election to the revolutionary convention entitled him to a seat in the Virginia House of Delegates, which convened in October 1776. As a member of the Committee on Religion, he worked closely with Thomas Jefferson, who led the drive to disestablish the publicly-supported Anglican Church in Virginia. Other committee work involved Madison in matters more directly related to the revolutionary cause. In carrying out his official duties, he exhibited a learned and agile mind, a facility for expression, and an ardent patriotism that did not go unnoticed among his fellow delegates. Yet when a confident Madison stood for re-election in April 1777, the voters turned him out: the result of his failure to actively campaign and his refusal to engage in the time-honored custom of plying voters with intoxicating drink. This sobering experience was an early lesson for young Madison: if he wanted a role in shaping the new nation's destiny, he would have to periodically play the political game.

Despite the snub from his neighbors, Madison was active in the revolutionary county government. Then in November 1777, he was elected to the Council of State, a small body which, under the new constitution, shared executive functions with the governor. During his tenure on the Council, Madison was immersed in a wide variety of matters, ranging from organizing the state militia and combating subversion, to securing Virginia's western land titles and supervising public finances. His working relationship with Jefferson, which began when both served in the Assembly, was renewed when the latter was elected governor in June 1779. This second collaboration solidified what has been called "the most fruitful political partnership in American history." In conjunction with their similar backgrounds, the two men's mutuality of interests and compatibility of ideas formed the basis of a deep and abiding friendship that spanned a half-century.

In December 1779, an experienced and tested Madison was elected to Congress, but was kept from attending until March due to a long winter. In the interim he wrote an essay entitled "Money," in which he insightfully addressed the grave fiscal crisis that threatened to undermine the war effort. The upshot of the argument was that the government in Philadelphia needed greater powers to rescue the nation's sinking credit, especially the authority to lay and energy to collect taxes. After some initial hesitation, Madison openly advocated such measures in Congress, where he emerged as an industrious and respected leader. Between March 1780 and October 1783, he served

on numerous committees, and was entrusted with handling important matters of state. With the government near collapse, Madison
worked diligently, if not always successfully, to give weight and bal-
last to the foundering Congress. In March 1781 he drafted an
amendment declaring that the Confederation government had an "implicit" right to employ physical coercion under the provision in the
Articles "that every state shall abide by the determinations of the
United States in Congress." The measure died in committee, but it
testified to Madison's conviction that the critical problems facing the
beleaguered republic demanded *national* solutions.

The wave of troubles that threatened to engulf Congress during the
Revolutionary War did not recede with the British invader after Yorktown.
Even with the enemy at the door, the bonds of union had strained under
fits of obduracy and shortsightedness on the part of Congress, the states,
and the people themselves. Now, with the immediate threat removed,
the impulses to cooperation and self-restraint were notably dulled. Beset
with a host of new difficulties, the battle-scarred nation could ill-afford a
spirit of narrow localism to pervade its councils. Yet this very tendency
was encouraged in Congress, many of whose members were "appointees" of the state legislatures and, in some cases, acted under their
instructions. At times this made Congress resemble a body of ambassadors, which indeed it was insofar as the Articles affirmed that each state
retained its "sovereignty, freedom, and independence." For his part,
Madison never neglected the legitimate interests of his own state, but he
also recognized more clearly than most the existence of a *distinct* national interest that required the superintendence of a truly *national*
authority. Vesting Congress with the necessary means to promote the
"national interest" was, however, more easily agreed to than affected.

In the face of such obstacles, Madison made a determined effort to
procure a reliable source of revenue for the Confederation's barren coffers. Under his leadership a plan of fiscal reform was drafted which
sought to encourage the cooperation of the states through a combination of carrots and sticks. The nationalist provisions of the plan,
however, were diluted or dropped, and Congress settled for a second
impost amendment, which was sent to the states for ratification in April
1783. In the accompanying address, Madison made an eloquent and
patriotic plea on behalf of adoption—an intransigent New York, however, failed to be moved, and the measure went the way of the first
impost. The provision for unanimity, as well as other features of the
Confederation, continued to frustrate the very purpose for which it
was created: an American Union, the very basis of "life, liberty, and the
pursuit of happiness." Before he left Congress in Fall 1783, Madison

concluded that nothing short of major structural reform could render the American Constitution "adequate to the exigencies of the Union." For the time, he restricted his energies to making the present system more functional, both in his official duties and as a leading voice for effective national government.

During his years in Congress Madison also became a staunch *continentalist* who embraced a vision (shared by Hamilton and Jay) of America as an expansive, "continental" power. Active in the area of foreign policy, he consistently defended the honor of Congress and the sovereignty of the republic against slights and threats from abroad. With notable skill and perseverance, he labored to secure the United States' claim to the trans-Appalachian West, its fishing rights off the northeast coast, and trading privileges with the European powers. He also worked out agreements whereby Virginia and other states ceded their western land titles to Congress, a step which greatly expanded the national domain, facilitated the ratification of the Articles, and gave the central government a potential source of income.

After an absence of nearly four years, Madison returned to Montpelier in December 1783. For the next three years he combined study and travel with the responsibilities of a delegate in the state legislature. Seasoned by his experience in Congress, Madison entered the Virginia House of Delegates in May 1784 with hopes of reforming the state constitution and carrying out a general revision of the laws which Jefferson and others had initiated in 1777. While constitutional reform was blocked, Madison made considerable headway on behalf of revising Virginia's statutes. He also helped defeat a controversial tax to support religious instruction. In his "Memorial and Remonstrance against Religious Assessments," Madison cogently enumerated the reasons for supporting religious liberty and the separation of church and state. Published in 1785 in response to an assessment bill, the popular "Remonstrance" had its intended effect, and has since become holy writ for defenders of complete church-state separation.

Active on a number of fronts at once, Madison also worked to stabilize Virginia's finances, promote interstate commerce, and bring the Old Dominion into compliance with federal requisitions, laws, and treaties. In the first and last cases, he was largely thwarted. He failed to prevent a one-year moratorium on taxes intended for the Confederation, and was frustrated in his efforts to repeal laws which barred British creditors from recovering pre-Revolutionary debts in Virginia courts. Like Hamilton, Madison stood firmly for property rights and openly opposed measures which violated the nation's treaty obligations. He did, however, help head off a movement to print paper money, a measure embraced by many debt-ridden farmers to alleviate their economic plight. The "mania" for paper had broken out in every state, seven of which issued currency for the purposes of borrowing and paying off debts. Trade wars between the states were already impeding the flow of commerce; now the "money wars" were draining the channels of credit. The cumulative effect was economic confusion and commercial paralysis. Printing money as an inflationary panacea—a common practice in the colonial period—was not only wrong in principle, Madison argued, but its practical effects were disastrous.

In the area of interstate trade and cooperation, Madison was ultimately more successful. In 1784 he laid the groundwork for the resolution of a dispute between Virginia and Maryland over navigation rights to the Potomac. Unable to attend the subsequent Mount Vernon Convention, Madison did obtain passage of a negotiated settlement in the General Assembly. With some evidence that cooperation could bear fruit, he inspired a motion in the legislature that endorsed a uniform system of interstate commerce under congressional regulation. To "examine" and "consider" such a step, Virginia invited the states to attend a convention in Annapolis. Discouraged by the poor response, Madison warmed to Hamilton's bold plan to turn the meeting's failure into a call for a future convention empowered to effect a more general reform. A few months later, Captain Shays' rag-tag army marched on the federal arsenal in Springfield, Massachusetts. Such was the uneven and turbulent road that led to Philadelphia.

In the months following the Annapolis Convention, Madison immersed himself in the study of government, history, and economics. Of special interest was the history of confederacies, which gave him added insight into the problems and pitfalls of federal systems. The notes he took on the subject served as a ready reference at the Federal Convention and were incorporated into some of his *Federalist* essays. They also supplied the raw material for "Vices of the Political System of the United States," written while Madison attended Congress in the spring of 1787. In this timely essay, he roundly denounced the selfish spirit of localism that animated state officials and their "agents" in Congress. The essay also included the first concrete expression of Madison's famous remedy for "factions," which he developed at greater length in *Federalist* No. 10.

When the man destined to be known as the "Father of the Constitution" arrived in Philadelphia in April 1787, he was thirty-six years old, and the premier authority on public affairs in the United States. In conjunction with his notable skill and experience as a legislator, Madison's impressive knowledge of history and political theory distinguished him even among what Jefferson (serving as minister to France at the time) compared to a gathering of "demi-gods." With a growing sense of personal destiny, Madison sedulously prepared for a leading role in the Convention by pouring over books and notes as the delegates trickled into town. Some weeks earlier he had outlined a plan of government, the essentials of which he hoped to substitute for the existing one. On May 29, four days after deliberations began, Edmund Randolph laid the so-called Virginia Plan before the assembled company. The plan (which was primarily the work of Madison) not only provided the framework for much of the subsequent debate; it was accepted as the essential structure around which the final document took shape. A major departure from the Articles, which vested all power in a unicameral Congress, the Virginia Plan called for a national government composed of three separate branches, including a bicameral legislature. The people would elect the lower house, which in turn would elect the upper house from among its own members. Representation in both chambers would be based on the free population or amount of taxes paid; a sharp deviation from the principle of state equality that had prevailed since the first Continental Congress.

The corollary to this profound structural change was a broad and unspecified grant of power "to legislate in all cases to which the separate States are incompetent." To insure the supremacy of national authority, the proposed congress could nullify state laws contrary to the constitution and/or acts of the general government. The national legislature was also authorized to select the executive, who would possess a qualified veto over the acts of that body. The national judiciary would be appointed by the upper house, and federal judges would enjoy life tenure on good behavior. Proposed terms for the lower and upper houses of the legislature were three and seven years respectively. The executive would sit for seven years, but was ineligible for re-election. The plan also called for an amendment procedure, and stipulated that the new constitution be ratified by state conventions elected directly by the people for that purpose.

On June 6, as delegates debated the method of electing the lower house, Madison rose to give what was probably his most important speech in the Convention. Foreshadowing the famous arguments of *Federalist* No. 10, he ingeniously reconciled concerns for stability and minority rights with popular consent and an increase in governmental powers. Only an "extended republic" in which the various interests or "factions" were diffused over a large territory, Madison argued, could accommodate these ostensibly conflicting values. Within such a framework, it was, for example, not only prudent, but "a clear principle of free government," that the lower house be directly elected by the people. Bolstered by separation of powers and a system of checks and balances, an "extended republic," Madison averred, was the best solution to the problem of preserving liberty and order in America.

The tentative adoption on June 13 of the amended Virginia Plan set off a storm of protest by delegates who viewed its provisions as "totally novel" and beyond the mandate of the Convention. In particular, opponents objected to the plan's provisions for representation, which threatened to "swallow up" the smaller states. On June 15 they rallied behind the so-called New Jersey Plan, which aimed to strengthen national authority, but retained the principle of state equality in a unicameral Congress.

After Hamilton's provocative speech of June 18, Madison rose in opposition to the New Jersey Plan. In masterly fashion, he highlighted its inadequacies, exposed many of the delegates' fears as groundless, and warned of the dire consequences of failing to establish a sufficiently strong union. With Hamilton's plan at one end of the political spectrum, and the New Jersey Plan at the other, the Virginia Plan was recast as a moderate solution to the country's problems. While a number of issues remained to be settled, the question of representation was far and away the most contentious; indeed it nearly sank the Convention. Madison was among those who insisted that representation on any other basis but population or wealth was contrary to fairness and patently undemocratic. Moreover, the large states would never accept the principle of state equality. Small state delegates were equally adamant in their opposition to proportional representation for both houses of the legislature. Deadlocked and on the verge of breaking up, the Convention assigned the matter to a committee, which recommended that each state be given an equal voice in the upper chamber, while retaining population as the basis for representation in the lower house. On July 16, over the objections of Madison and others, the Convention adopted the measure known as the "Great Compromise": the most formidable obstacle to "a more perfect union" had narrowly been overcome.

Madison continued to oppose the compromise on principle, but ultimately acquiesced when it became apparent that the decision would not be reversed. From this point forward, he became more cautious in the matter of granting powers to the national government, and supported the decision to replace the open-ended grant of legislative authority in the Virginia Plan with a limited number of "delegated" powers. His most important contribution, however, was on behalf of the principles of separation of powers and checks and balances. Madison specifically underscored the necessity of making both the executive and judicial branches independent of the legislature, which by its very nature tended to predominate. To this end he argued for popular election of the president, opposed exclusive legislative appointment of judges, and proposed vesting the veto power in a revisory council composed of the president and supreme court justices. While Madison's proposals were not always adopted, the underlying principles behind them were generally adhered to by a majority of delegates. As the most articulate champion of these principles, Madison is rightly credited with being the preeminent member of the Convention.

A few days after signing the Constitution, Madison left Philadelphia for New York, where he intended to serve in Congress and work on behalf of ratification. A few weeks after his arrival, he was approached by Hamilton and Jay, who sought his collaboration for *The Federalist* project. Madison's first essay, the now-famous No. 10, appeared in the New York press on November 22. Before the year was out, he had contributed another four papers, No. 14 and Nos. 18–20, the latter three written with the help of Hamilton's notes. After a brief respite, Madison struck off twenty-two consecutive essays (Nos. 37–58) in the first two months of 1788. His final contributions (Nos. 62 and 63) appeared just before he left New York in early March.

Initially, Madison had no intention of serving in his home state's ratifying convention, considering it impolitic to sit in judgment of a document he himself had helped draft. Yet rising opposition to the Constitution in Virginia led him to reconsider, and in late March he was elected as a delegate. In the two-months prior to the Convention, Madison worked to strengthen the hand of pro-ratification forces in a number of ways. First, he corresponded with Federalists in other states, offering advice on strategy. He also conceded that a bill of rights should be added to the Constitution (a major objection of its opponents), but only following adoption. Third, he attempted to dispel fears that the new government would acquiesce in Spain's closure of the Mississippi to American commerce (a major concern of residents of western Virginia). Closer to home, he continued the delicate task of bringing the influential Edmund Randolph (who had not signed the Constitution) into the Federalist camp. Madison also had numerous copies of *The Federalist* distributed to the convention delegates.

When Madison arrived in Richmond in early June for the opening session, eight states had already given their approval to the Constitution. This fact, however, made little impression on Antifederalists in Virginia, who were determined to block ratification at all costs. The Convention as a whole was evenly divided, save a handful of uncommitted delegates, whose votes would determine the outcome. Leading the opposition was George Mason, author of the Virginia Declaration of Rights (1776), and the indefatigable Patrick Henry. Joining Madison on the side of adoption were Revolutionary War hero Henry "Light Horse Harry" Lee, future Supreme Court Chief Justice John Marshall, and Virginia governor Edmund Randolph, who had finally succumbed to Madison's powerful arguments. In the three weeks of debate before the final vote, Madison made a series of brilliant speeches in which he demolished the arguments of Henry, exposed the "imbecility" of the Articles, defended the specific provisions of the Constitution, and warned of the grave consequences of disunion. As Hamilton would do in Poughkeepsie, Madison drew readily from *The Federalist* in stating the case for adoption. He also put to rest the notion that the absent Jefferson opposed ratification, and later announced that George Washington (with whom Madison had developed a close working relationship) was solidly behind it. Along with these revelations, Madison's forceful arguments swayed enough of the undecided to secure the margin of victory. On June 25 Virginia voted for ratification 89 to 79.

# *John Jay*
# *(1745–1829)*

JOHN JAY, the descendent of French Huguenot emigrés, was born in New York in 1745. Serious and quick to learn, Jay entered King's College at the age of fourteen, following three years of study under Protestants in France. Upon graduating, he studied law, was admitted to the bar in 1768, and within a few years had an active practice. In 1773 his defense of a Westchester mayor, whom royal officials hoped to force from office, gained him the attention of Whig leaders in New York. Jay lost the case, but his support of American authority and a broader suffrage (the Crown had alleged "illegal" voting), won him respect and popularity.

In the spring of 1774, Jay married Sarah Livingston, daughter of William Livingston, a prominent lawyer and leader of the anti-British forces in New York. The marriage, like Hamilton's, enhanced Jay's social prestige and political clout. Not long afterwards, Jay was elected to the Committee of Fifty-One, an extralegal body hastily formed after British warships sealed off Boston Harbor. His first important assignment was drafting a letter calling for a meeting of provincial representatives to coordinate the resistance movement. When the first Continental Congress convened in Philadelphia the following September, John Jay was seated as a delegate, and was numbered among the moderates who showed greater caution and restraint in opposition to Parliament and Crown than their more radical compatriots. After Congress adopted the defiant Suffolk Resolves, Jay rallied support for Joseph Galloway's conciliatory "Plan of Union," which stopped short of demanding independence. The proposal failed by a single vote, and the radicals, heartened by their victory, had the tally expunged from the record. This setback was countered by Jay's rousing "Address to the People of Great Britain," which won him respect and influence among his colleagues.

Returning to New York, Jay worked successfully to moderate the transition from royal to revolutionary government and was elected to state office. As a member of the Committee of Inspection, he gained a reputation as a vigorous enforcer of bans on the importation and sale of British goods. Jay was next elected to a state convention which picked New York's delegates to the second Continental Congress. When that body met in May 1775, Jay was again in attendance, and quickly emerged as one of the leaders of the moderate wing. By this time fighting had broken out in Massachusetts and revolutionary governments throughout the colonies (including Congress) were preparing for war. Though it was clear to most patriots that there could be no turning back, Jay and other moderates held out hope of reconciliation, making one last effort to facilitate a peaceful settlement. The resultant "Olive Branch Petition," addressed to His Majesty, George III, was rejected out of hand: the King was in no mood to conciliate his "deluded" American subjects.

Even after news of the failed peace initiative, Jay remained a reluctant rebel. Elected to New York's provincial legislature in the spring of 1776, he encouraged local patriots to assume the functions of government, but also sponsored a resolution prohibiting the state's delegation in Congress from voting for a formal break with England. Only after the Declaration of Independence was proclaimed did Jay fully embrace the revolutionary cause. Before the year was out, he was organizing military defenses, running an intelligence operation, and drafting a constitution for New York. Adopted by the provincial assembly with some alterations, Jay's constitution broadened the suffrage, weakened executive power, and expanded religious toleration. Shortly thereafter, Jay was appointed chief justice of New York's high court, but resigned within a year to rejoin Congress. After serving as that body's president for several months, he was sent to Spain to secure a treaty similar to the alliance made with France in 1778. After more than two years of fruitless talks, Jay joined the American delegation in Paris for peace negotiations with Britain. Entanglements with France, complications involving Spain, and the intransigence of the British commissioners delayed the proceedings. Acting on his own authority, Jay effected a breakthrough via private discussions with British agents without consulting the French commissioners. Having facilitated serious negotiations, Jay went on to play a central role in fashioning the Treaty of Paris (1783), which officially ended the war and recognized America's independence.

After some four years in Europe, Jay returned to an enthusiastic reception in New York City. Reelected to Congress in 1784, he shortly resigned to become Secretary for Foreign Affairs, a position for which his tenure on the "Secret Correspondence" committee and experience abroad left him well-suited. In this capacity, Jay became the single most important public officer in the country, assuming an unofficial status as prime minister. As foreign secretary, he entered into negotiations with Spain over the unresolved issues of free navigation of the Mississippi and bilateral trade. Congress wanted an accord securing both, but Jay, thinking the waterway would not be of use for some time (and aware that America could not force Spain to open it), was willing to sacrifice the one (at least temporarily) for the sake of the other. Such a compromise was welcome to northeastern commercial interests, but provoked shouts of protest among residents of the southwest who considered control of the lower Mississippi vital to their prosperity. After the adoption of the Constitution in 1788, negotiations with the Spanish envoy ceased. In the midst of these activities, Jay was appointed a trustee of the manumission society which Alexander Hamilton had helped to form, and later became its president.

From the time of his conversion to the cause of Independence, Jay was a confirmed nationalist who grew increasingly committed to greater centralization in government. Upon his return from Europe, he joined a growing chorus of prominent voices calling for a convention to revise the hapless Articles. Privately he went so far as to recommend (as Hamilton had done in the Federal Convention) reducing the troublesome states to administrative districts of the national authority. After the Constitution was signed, however, he supported the compromise hammered out in Philadelphia: first, by joining Hamilton in the "Publius" project, then by penning the influential "Address to the People of the State of New York," and finally, by his vital role at the Poughkeepsie ratifying convention.

Had Jay not suffered a disabling attack of rheumatism, he would have no doubt contributed more to the total output of *The Federalist*. As it was, he authored papers No. 2 through No. 5, took ill, and then assumed the guise of Publius only once more (No. 64). In the former essays, Jay underscored the "naturalness" of a firm union of the American people, and its necessity for ensuring the security of the nation. In his final effort, he defended the Constitution's provisions for treaty-making and offered some sage observations on diplomacy.

# The Identity of "Publius"

EVEN BEFORE Hamilton's untimely death in 1804, the identity of "Publius" was fairly well known. The specific authorship of some of the papers, however, remained a point of conjecture for many years; in no small part due to conflicting attributions by the authors themselves. In the 1940s, however, Douglas Adair firmly established the authorship of the contested essays. And while this may be of some consequence to the specialist, it is largely irrelevant to the content of the papers themselves, which read as if they came from a single pen.* This manifest continuity is largely attributable to the singularity of purpose which gave rise to Hamilton's project: to defend and explain the Constitution in hopes of ratification. That Hamilton and Madison refrained from expressing the more divergent aspects of their respective political views is clear from the records of the Constitutional debates. As noted above, neither man came near to embracing all of the final document's provisions.

Still, some overly subtle scholars have tried to use the authorship of the papers (as well as the two men's subsequent politics) to drive a wedge between the ideas of Hamilton and Madison as they appear in *The Federalist*. There are perhaps some differences in emphasis; namely, Hamilton underscoring the need for "energy" in government, and Madison highlighting the "limited" scope of national authority. Yet even here numerous counter-examples must frustrate any attempt to sharply distinguish the authors' respective contributions. In fact, what distinctions do exist in *The Federalist* owe more to a division of labor than to a divergence of views. For all intents and purposes, "Publius" speaks with one voice.

---

*For readers interested in the authorship of the individual essays, the following list provides a key:

Alexander Hamilton, Nos. 1, 6–9, 11–13, 15–17, 21–36, 59–61, 65–85
James Madison, Nos. 10, 14, 18–20, 37–58, 62–63
John Jay, Nos. 2–5, 64

# The Science of Publius: Method & Prescription in *The Federalist*

T HE SCIENTIFIC REVOLUTION'S enormous impact on traditional patterns of thought and culture is certainly among the most profound developments in the course of Western Civilization. Today, centuries after the first great discoveries, the pervasiveness of science has become so manifest, and the inevitability of its triumph so apparent, that it is hard to imagine a time when science (as we understand it) was ignored, neglected, or resisted. Yet it was in just such an age that the modern scientific spirit first ventured out into the broader world of ideas: into philosophy, politics, ethics, education, history, medicine, and even theology. Indeed, by the end of the seventeenth century, each of these "disciplines," while retaining some vestiges of the medieval past, had been indelibly stamped by modern science. Given the "obscurantism" of the Middle Ages on one hand, and the precision, universality, and explanatory power of the "new science" on the other, this could hardly have been otherwise. Science was not only persuasive in the intellectual sense, it was eminently useful, and, as such, gave rise to notions of control, progress, and mastery. For these reasons, science instilled its practitioners and popularizers with a spirit of confidence. Science, more than any other factor, contributed to the West's "recovery of nerve."[1]

# Intellectual Background:
# The Mature Enlightenment

IN HINDSIGHT, many of the early efforts to place such disciplines as meta-
physics, ethics and politics on a strictly scientific basis appear quaint.[2] By
the second half of the eighteenth century, however, many admirers of
the scientific method had become more mindful of its limits when directly applied to man and society. In the seventeenth century "natural
philosophy" had meant science, and natural science was largely inter-
changeable with "philosophy." Yet before the end of the eighteenth
century the two had begun to noticeably diverge. Less than a century
later, science and philosophy were often viewed as antagonists. Today
the two disciplines have become so specialized that an individual with
the learning of a Bacon or a Descartes, a Kant or a Goethe might have
trouble finding work in either! Yet there was a time, between the extremes of the early enthusiasts and our contemporary relativists, when
the spirit of science was *prudently* applied to the broader social world—a
time when many of the best minds firmly believed that a combination of
reason, experience, and a basic understanding of man's nature could render accurate and useful generalizations on the whole array of human
activity. This was the time of the *mature* Enlightenment, roughly the
half-century before the French Revolution.

The outlook of the representatives of this age, the *philosophes*, was
rooted in a shared set of assumptions regarding the structure of Nature
and the nature of man.[3] The early scientists had demonstrated that
nature was continuous, uniform, and governed by immutable laws. Nature, therefore, was *intelligible*, and in some cases, predictable. As with
Darwin's discoveries two centuries later, the temptation to apply these
findings to man and society proved irresistible, and not infrequently,
resulted in similarly crude effects. In time, however, the application of
scientific concepts and methods to the social and humane sciences became more selective and sophisticated. The initial premise, however,
remained intact: while specific *behaviors* might be modified through
education and habit, the essential features of man's *nature* were universal and fixed. On the surface this did not always appear the case. For
example, men were different in appearance, worshiped different gods,
and lived under different social and political arrangements. Yet to many
of the *philosophes* these differences were more apparent than real; they

were accidental, not fundamental differences. In all essentials, men, past and present, were the same.

What, then, are the basic traits which men at all times, in all societies and under all governments allegedly possess? Most fundamental is the impulse to *self-preservation*, the native desire to secure one's own well-being. The *philosophes* also agreed that all men desire *liberty*—at a minimum freedom from the arbitrary will of another, at best, the removal of all impediments to his mental and moral betterment. A third characteristic, implied by the other two, was self-love or *self-interest*. Thomas Hobbes (1588–1679), convinced that the "natural" interplay of these qualities *among* men was mutually destructive, insisted that only the dread-awe of an absolute "sovereign" could ensure any real security or continuity in human affairs. The *philosophes*, while never in strict agreement on the overall character and prospects of humanity, generally accorded mankind a significantly greater native capacity for *sociability* than Hobbes. They also tended to agree (again contra Hobbes) that man possessed a *moral sense*, an innate understanding that certain actions are right and others wrong. Finally, and most importantly, there was a general consensus that all men had a *capacity for reason*. Whatever the differences in the relative strength or exercise of the rational faculty among *individual* men (and these were readily admitted) there was little doubt that the faculty itself was (excepting infants, lunatics, and the impaired) universal.

"Reason," in its various forms, was, arguably, *the* central idea of the Enlightenment. The triumphs of science in the sixteenth and seventeenth centuries—those of Copernicus, Galileo and Newton—had been conquests of *reason*. The scientifically-minded *philosophes* looked on the achievements of these men with awe and admiration, struck no less by the formidable powers of man's intellect than by the discoveries themselves. They paid homage to both by making reason (or *reasonableness*) their rallying cry, aligning themselves with the scientific movement, and by emulating scientific method. The *philosophes* were eminently impressed by the discovery that the world (and perhaps everything in it) obeyed a set of basic *natural* laws. The universe was not only intelligible—it was rational; indeed, it was intelligible for this very reason. This, at least, could be said with confidence in the case of inanimate nature: the "operation" of individuals and society, however, was quite a different matter. Applied reason might render the workings of man and society "intelligible," but this said little regarding the "rationality" of the one or the "reasonableness" of the other. Indeed, it was in their crusade against the persistence of "irrationalism," in a less than fully-enlightened eighteenth century, that the European *philosophes* gained their reputation as pointed critics and scathing satirists.

The principal achievement of the *philosophes*, then, was not primarily in the realm of discovery, but rather in the broadening and deepening of the rational, "scientific" attitude. More specifically, their contribution centered on the application of "reason" to such disparate spheres as religion, government, ethics, education, and economics. These too could be rendered intelligible, it was argued, for the world of man also partook of the natural order of things. The difference, of course, was that whereas natural laws might be said to apply to the physical and human realms alike, such laws were clearly violable in the case of man. This paradox, however, did not much trouble the *philosophes*, many of whom rather loosely identified the "rational" with the "natural." The adoption of this outlook not only provided the basis for a "scientific" (secular-empiricist-naturalistic) approach to man and society, it also contained a standard for measuring their health and progress; a standard many *philosophes* believed was both *objective* and *universal*. Such beliefs rested on the assumption that the principle of "natural law" was not limited to "hard" science, but was applicable to society, morals, and politics. It was also necessary to assume that this expanded notion of natural law was capable of being known by all men through the unaided faculty of reason. Consequently, natural law concepts and value-laden references to "Nature" figure prominently in the writings of the period, serving as an intellectual pillar for the *philosophes'* belief in the existence of moral, political, and even aesthetic "truths."

These aspects of Enlightenment thought were the common property of inhabitants on both sides of the Atlantic. Historically speaking, the main difference was that "the Old World imagined the Enlightenment and the New World realized it. The Old World invented it, formulated it, and agitated it; America absorbed it, reflected it, and institutionalized it."[4] The culmination of this process took the form of a series of political and constitutional innovations by thirteen former colonies of British North America. Indeed, it was in the *science of politics*—not in art, music, literature, or philosophy—that the American Enlightenment reached its zenith and made its most distinctive contribution. The enduring legacy of this epoch-making achievement is reflected in the Declaration of Independence, the state and federal constitutions, and the Bill of Rights. In these documents the Enlightenment (as far as the "science of government" and the "rights of man" were concerned) celebrated its greatest triumph.[5]

# The Emergence of "The Federalist"

BECAUSE THE Founding documents contain *statements* rather than *explanations* of the leading principles of the American creed, the workings of the Enlightenment spirit is not immediately apparent in them. Consequently, it has been suggested that the practical-minded American Founders lacked a political philosophy altogether.[6] In reality, the relative lack of interest in abstract political theory among the Founders (and Americans in general) signified neither the absence of a "philosophy" nor an admission that their political activity was bereft of a theoretical core. True, their speculations rarely ascended to the realm of pure theory, but given their practical tasks, this was more a virtue than a defect. After all, in America the major political thinkers were among the leading statesmen: men actively engaged in fighting for independence, framing constitutions, and filling important posts in the new governments. It was to these concrete ends, not to politics in the abstract, that they directed their theorizing. Yet to say that the Founders simply "subordinated" theory to practice would be misleading, even contradictory. More accurately, their theories were built upon firmly-held political *principles*, the lessons of *experience*, and the parameters of the *possible*. This is nowhere more evident than in the most celebrated political work of this or any other period in American history—*The Federalist*.[7]

The brainchild of Alexander Hamilton, and the joint product of Hamilton, James Madison, and John Jay, *The Federalist* first began appearing *seriatim* in New York City newspapers a little over a month after the signing of the Constitution in Philadelphia.[8] Often writing at breakneck speed, the trio published some seventy-seven essays or "papers" between October 1787 and March 1788. (The final eight first appeared as part of the second volume of *The Federalist* published in May 1788.) The practical and immediate object of the papers was to persuade "the People of the State of New York" to ratify the proposed Constitution.[9] But "Publius," their pseudonymous author, was acting as more than a mere publicist. In the process of trumpeting the virtues of the proposed Constitution (and defending it from its detractors), he also explained its inner workings and identified the likely effects of its adoption. Indeed, *The Federalist* is best known as an authoritative commentary on the Constitution and may still be profitably read as such. And yet it is more than a commentary. For in seeking to instruct and persuade, Publius, almost inadvertently, constructs a theory of politics: "almost," because the very nature of the task required a degree of theoretical elaboration. The authors of *The Federalist*, however, clearly felt a need to go beyond the bare minimum. In fact, for all their "realism" and practicality, Hamilton, Madison, and Jay gave greater scope to their philosophical tendencies in these essays than anywhere else in their public writings. In doing so they created not just a partisan tract or a learned commentary, but a *bona fide* work of political theory.

While never falling into obscurity, in more recent years *The Federalist* has been the subject of renewed interest as witnessed by the flood of books and articles dedicated to its explication. And yet many histories of political thought pass over Publius without so much as a word.[10] That such surveys tend to ignore American political thought in general is no doubt the chief reason for this omission. The "hybrid" nature of the papers themselves is perhaps an additional cause of neglect. In any case, *The Federalist* has never attained the kind of status as a work of political *theory* that has traditionally been accorded to such classics as Hobbes' *Leviathan*, Locke's *Second Treatise of Government*, and Rousseau's *Social Contract*. Publius does not, as these authors do, engage in foundational discussions of natural law, sovereignty, individual rights, political obligation, or property.[11] The nature of his task, as well as the broad consensus on these matters among Americans, alleviated the need to do so. The absence of such discussions, therefore, should not be viewed as a defect or a regrettable lacuna. Simply stated, *The Federalist* (apart from its immediate purpose) *is* a genuine work of political theory; one whose merits have elevated the names of Madison and Hamilton to that select company of *classical* political authors.

# A Question of Method

AN ENCOMIUM ON *The Federalist*, however fitting, is not the subject of this essay. Rather, I intend to underscore the theoretical nature of the work as reflected in its authors' *method* of political analysis. A secondary concern involves the *relation* between this method and the authors' defense of certain "undemocratic" features of the Constitution. As will be shown, Publius' method is founded upon appeals to (1) reason, (2) history or "experience," and (3) human nature. Typically, such appeals emerge as the by-product (rather than the subject) of analysis, and at times his assumptions are only implicitly stated. Yet in approaching the "science of

Publius" on this basis, a clear pattern begins to emerge; one that not merely identifies *The Federalist* as the work of American *philosophes*, but confirms it as the Enlightenment's supreme achievement in political thought.[12]

The conviction that truly "useful" (explanatory and prescriptive) political theory requires a prudent application of reason, insight into human nature, and a felicity for interpreting the past, is apparent in nearly all eighty-five of the papers. A classic statement of this view was made by Hamilton in an address at the New York ratifying convention. Here the principal "Publius" summarizes the method of *The Federalist*:

> The means of accomplishing [the establishment of a republican government] become the most important study which can inter-est mankind. It is our duty to examine all those means with peculiar attention, and to choose the best and most effectual. *It is our duty to draw from nature, from reason, from examples, the best principles of policy, and to pursue and apply them in the formation of our government.* We should contemplate and compare the sys-tems, which, in this examination, come under our view; distinguish with a careful eye, the defects and excellences of each, and, discarding the former, incorporate the latter, as far as cir-cumstances will admit, into our constitution.[13]

*The Federalist* was, of course, written after the Constitution was signed, but its authors defended that document by recourse to the same three principles. As a work of synthesis aimed at informing and persuading, these principles are treated neither separately nor "formally," but inter-dependently. For it is *reason* (broadly conceived), which gives insight into the political implications of *human nature*, and reason which renders the *lessons of history* intelligible. Reason, nature, and experience, then, are three legs of a stool that cannot stand with one leg missing. Still, these "legs" remain conceptually distinct and may be duly examined in their own right. In the present case, this means observing the manner in which reason, history, and human nature inform the method and reflect the aims of Publius.

# The Rule of Reason

IF ONE WERE to describe *The Federalist* in a single word, it would be *reasonable*; and this characterization applies equally to the work's tone, method, and observations.[14] Given the author's assumption that government and politics are amenable to "scientific" treatment, the emphasis on reason is only fitting. That Publius views politics as a genuine science, which like other sciences, had been advanced substantially in modern times, is made explicit by Hamilton:

> The science of politics . . . like most other sciences has received great improvement. The efficacy of various principles is now well understood, which were either not known at all, or imperfectly known to the ancients. (No. 9)[15]

Just as Kepler had discovered the laws of motion and Newton the law of gravity, the American *philosophes* had made "wholly new discoveries" in the realm of government.[16] As we have seen, the basis for this belief was the notion that man and society, like nature itself, operated according to intelligible "laws." A parallel, therefore, existed between the deductive and empirical sciences on the one hand and the social sciences on the other. The correspondence was obviously not exact, but as the following passage illustrates, it was deemed strong enough to justify the claim of direct kinship:

> In disquisitions of every kind there are certain primary truths or first principles upon which all subsequent reasoning must depend. These contain an internal evidence, which antecedent to all reflection or combination commands the assent of the mind. Where it produces not this effect, it must proceed either from some defect or disorder in the organs of perception, or from the influence of some strong interest, or passion, or prejudice. Of this nature are the maxims of geometry . . . Of the same nature are these other maxims of ethics and politics. (No. 31)

Here, in the most philosophical of the papers, Publius unequivocally embraces the notion that politics (and ethics) may be reduced to a science.[17] Accordingly, the first principles of politics, like those of geometry, are self-evident or axiomatic. For example, there are the "self-evident truths" contained in the Declaration of Independence; i.e., that all men are created equal and possess an inalienable right to "life, liberty, and the pursuit of happiness." Other "truths" of a self-evident nature concern government more directly; e.g., "that the means ought to be proportioned to the end; that every power ought to be commensurate with its object; that there ought to be no limitation of a power destined to effect a purpose which is itself incapable of limitation." (No. 31) Such "axioms" also serve as the basis for making deductions, or "direct inferences," which produce knowledge of a more specific kind; e.g., that to protect man's natural rights "governments are instituted among men." And while it cannot be maintained that the "principles of moral and political knowledge have . . . the same degree of certainty with those of mathematics," they are nonetheless "so obvious in themselves, and so agreeable to the natural and unsophisticated dictates of common sense," that they literally compel the mind's assent.[18] Such principles, then, are *true*.

The difference between "hard" science and political science lies not primarily in their divergent objects of enquiry, but in the "abstracted" and impersonal nature of the former and the tangible and "felt" quality of the latter. Men will readily concur to the theorems of science, both simple and abstruse, for such matters do not "stir up and put into motion the unruly passions of the human heart. But in the sciences of morals and politics," which do just that, "men are found far less tractable." (No. 31) This fact is not, however, altogether regrettable; indeed, caution and reserve are necessary safeguards to the dangers of submissiveness and credulity. Carried too far, however, skepticism "may degenerate into obstinateness, perverseness or disingenuity." Disputes over moral and political principles, then, are not due to the inherent subjectivity of politics and morality *per se*: the source of disagreement lies more "in the passions and prejudices of the reasoner than in the subject."[19] Hence, major divergences in morals and politics are neither inevitable nor necessary, but result primarily from a deficiency of *reason*, a lack of disinterestedness, or a failure of men to "give their own understanding fair play."

That some men are guilty of such lapses much of the time, and all men some of the time, in no way weakens Publius' faith in the objectivity of certain moral and political "truths"—some self-evident or axiomatic, others inferred from experience, still others rooted in the nature of man. The failure of men and governments to conform to these truths in no way nullifies their validity. Publius does concede, however, that not all such truths are self-evident, deducible from "axioms," or even discernible by common sense. Indeed, as one moves from general to more specific political principles, and from theory to practice, the possibility for "error" increases substantially. There is, then, a scale of political knowledge that begins with the "plainest and simplest truths" (No. 33) and stretches gossamer-like to the most qualified probabilities. For example, that power should be separated is axiomatic (No. 47), but the best means of doing so strains the very limits of political wisdom. (No. 37) Unlike some of their contemporaries, Madison, Hamilton, and Jay held no illusions regarding the limits of political reason. They believed in the existence of moral and political truth, but they did not maintain that human reason was, in all cases, capable of its discovery. In addition to "the imperfection of the human faculties" (No. 37)—including the imprecision and ambiguities of language—political questions are obscured by their inherent complexity and by the difficulty of foreseeing "indirect and remote" consequences. (No. 10) Despite a profound attachment to reason and a reverence for the "divine science of politics," Publius never loses sight of the all-too-human defects of our nature. More than once he cautions readers against unrealistic "expectations and hopes from the efforts of human sagacity." (No. 37) This admonition not only indicates a recognition of intellectual limitations; it signifies, for Publius, the verdict of history and a judgment on mankind.

# The Oracle of Experience

IN THE LATTER stages of the Federal Convention, John Dickinson reminded his colleagues that "Experience must be our only guide. Reason may mislead us."[20] Few words could better capture the methodology of *The Federalist* than these. Indeed, its authors considered "reason"—abstracted from time, place, and circumstances—not only inadequate, but positively mischievous to the tasks of political construction.[21] This is seen, for example, in the recurring broadsides leveled at "those idle theories" concocted by "closet" political thinkers. No less than demagogues who prey on men's ignorance and passions, "[t]heoretic politicians," with their excessive "abstraction and refinements . . . lead men astray from the plainest paths of reason and conviction." (No. 12)[22]

It is not theorizing *per se* that Publius condemns, but theorizing that is at once abstract and ahistorical. In fact, theoretical reasoning is an assumed feature of any constructive discussion of political principles. In this sense, *The Federalist* is itself a work of theory, albeit one that is empirically-minded, historically-informed and practically-directed. In most cases, "theoretic reasoning" is of genuine value only when "qualified by the lessons of practice." (No. 43)[23] Hence, Publius' impatience with "those political doctors, whose sagacity disdains the admonitions of experimental instruction." (No. 28)

In this context "experimental instruction" means "experience" and experience means, primarily, *history*—both recent and remote. When Dickinson asserted that "experience" must guide the deliberations in Philadelphia, he was using the term in this sense. In fine, he was suggesting that the past (or a select part of it) was directly relevant to the present task of establishing a new government. This view of history—that the past could be of considerable utility to statesmen—was consciously shared by the Framers; in fact, it was the predominant view of the time. For many of the *philosophes* history was, in Lord Bolingbrook's famous phrase, "philosophy teaching by examples." It was in this spirit that the Founders studied the past—not as an end in itself, but as a kind of *oracle* one might consult for the purposes of statecraft, and specifically, constitution-making. Due to this orientation, their mature historical inquiries were necessarily selective and often fused with their political activities. In the words of Ralph Waldo Emerson, they employed history "to give value to the present hour and its duty." Given the gravity of this duty, the Founders earnestly aimed to interpret the lessons of the past correctly, and as men of reason, believed they could. More than a few were aware that failure to do so would doom not only the American experiment in self-government, but imperil the cause of republicanism itself.[24] If any group of statesmen truly heeded Santayana's monitory proverb regarding the dangers of ignoring the past, it was the Framers of the Constitution. *The Federalist*, more than any other contemporary document, confirms that they did.

Publius' "use" of history, so characteristic of the Enlightenment, was made possible due to a set of shared assumptions regarding the nature of historical events and processes. The notion that human history operated according to certain principles or patterns was simply the corollary of natural law philosophy as applied to man's social activity. This ascription not only rendered the past more intelligible, it instilled history with meaning and relevance. And while philosopher-historians disputed the finer points of interpretation, few denied the existence of discernible (and therefore instructive) patterns in the past.

The historically-minded among the revolutionary generation (which includes nearly all the leading figures) were much less concerned with grand theory than with how the past could illuminate the political situation in America. For such practical purposes it was not necessary to determine, for instance, whether history was circular or linear, or if it was driven by mind, matter, or spirit.[25] It simply required a belief in discernible patterns of causality and a commensurability of past, present, and future events. That the authors of *The Federalist* held this view, "that what has so often happened, would under similar circumstances happen again" (No. 4), is palpably evident throughout the papers.[26] This notion or "use" of history constitutes (along with reason and human nature) a central component of *The Federalist*'s political science.

It would be misleading to suggest that Publius views the annals of mankind as a repository of practical wisdom capable of being ransacked for ready-made answers to specific political questions. On the other hand, he takes some notable liberties with the past and tends to underscore his "findings" with a rhetorical punch. *The Federalist* is, among other things, a work of political persuasion. This said, it remains the case that Madison, Hamilton, and Jay were convinced that history *was* relevant to the task of elucidating and defending systems of government, specifically the one set forth in the Constitution. While not always punctilious with the past, they were far from blind to the limits of historical analogy.[27] As shown above, Publius is quite willing to acknowledge the limits of political reason; and despite some rhetorical flourishes to the contrary, this is no less the case with history. Just as there is a table of political truth that starts with the self-evident axioms and stretches to the remotest speculations, there is a table of historical truth as well.

That history *teaches* is, for Publius, indisputable. "Some portion of [political] knowledge," Madison affirms, "may no doubt be acquired in a man's closet." (No. 53) That the "lessons of experience" are *relevant* is likewise assumed. For Americans in 1787–88 this meant consulting (1) the history of "popular" governments, ancient and modern; (2) the history of confederal systems, republican or otherwise; and, (3) the history of Great Britain, "which presents mankind with so many political lessons." (No. 56) Finally, and decisively, there was America's recent experience under the Articles of Confederation. The number of instances in which Publius draws on these histories to establish or reinforce a point is truly impressive. It is not the aim here to enumerate these. Generally speaking, however, the past is used in *The Federalist* to accomplish two broad goals: first, to highlight the inviable nature of the Confederation and the dire consequences of rejecting the proposed Constitution; and second, to assuage the anxiety of those who feared that a strong central government would be inimical to their liberties. In carrying out this plan, Publius invokes history as an impartial judge whose "sentences" are less concerned with abstract justice than with prudential truth. History, then, is an "oracle," and Publius pronounces many of its judgments with notable aplomb.

Again, it is never asserted that "experience" is an infallible guide to political wisdom. Moreover, "history" was conspicuously silent on the most fundamental question of all: the viability of an untried, "experimental" form of government. Indeed, the uniqueness of America's situation was not lost on the Framers, who recognized that the lack of precedent in establishing an "extended" federal republic limited the applicability of the past to the untried part of their task.[28] Publius does, however, insist that history affords the prudent observer a considerable stock of relevant knowledge, some of which is indispensable to the task of erecting a just and stable republic. History, while not always an authoritative guide, remains "the least fallible" one (No. 6), and "where its responses are unequivocal, they ought to be conclusive and sacred." (No. 20)[29]

On the whole, the use of history in *The Federalist* is remarkably effective, and relatively circumspect given the partisan context of the ratification struggle. And while such "naive" and value-laden historiography would not likely pass muster with contemporary historians, few would deny Publius' basic premise: that "experience is the parent of wisdom." (No. 72)

# The Nature of Man

IT IS A common observation that all theories of government are, either implicitly or explicitly, based on a conception of human nature. The political theory developed in *The Federalist* is no exception.[30] "But what is government itself," Madison observes, "but the greatest of all reflections on human nature." (No. 51)[31] No less than Plato, Hobbes or Rousseau, Publius grounds his theory of (republican) government in the nature of man, and the link between the two is apparent throughout the papers. More specifically, references to human nature (like those to history) are used by the authors to support nearly every major contention, and a number of minor ones too. One will not, as noted above, find in *The Federalist* a systematic treatment of human nature, nor meet with discussions of natural law, the state of nature, or the social contract. The existence of natural rights is assumed, as is the Lockean theory of the origin and role of government.[32] Acceptance of these tenets did not, however, imply a blind preference for republican (or federated) government. Men might have a natural right to "life, liberty, and estate," but Publius was acutely aware that such rights were not by definition more secure under a "popular" government than under a "mixed," or even a monarchical one.

Given the volatile history of "popular" governments, the burden of proof clearly fell on its defenders: unfortunately, America's untoward experience under the Articles gave them little to cheer about. On the contrary, it had (in Madison's words) "tainted the faith of most orthodox republicans."[33] As this "faith" was based on a generally favorable view of mankind's capacity for self-government, its questioning was a judgment on human nature with profound political implications. George Washington spoke volumes when he noted, "We have, probably, had too good an opinion of human nature in forming our confederation."[34] Washington's remark, uttered in the wake of Shays' Rebellion, implied a modification of this "opinion," and thereby raised a question no sincere republican could ignore: Were men, given their natural composition and propensities, capable of governing themselves? Was liberty compatible with order and a respect for individual rights, including those of the minority? The men of '76 had staked their lives, their fortunes, and their sacred honor on an affirmative answer to these questions. The turbulence and strife that followed independence had shaken their convictions, but it did not change their minds. Rather, it convinced them of the necessity of modifying, not man's *nature*, but his *government*, in order to protect him against others and himself. The United States' first experiment in self-government had "taught mankind the necessity of auxiliary precautions." (No. 51) The absence of such "precautions" had threatened the blessings of liberty, and ultimately, liberty itself. The "solution" was to frame a government that would preserve the essentials of the social and commercial order without sacrificing republican principles. This was the monumental task assigned to the fifty-five men who assembled at the Pennsylvania State House in the spring and summer of 1787. It was their peculiar fate to determine "whether societies of men are really capable or not, of establishing good government from reflection and choice, or whether they are forever destined to depend, for their political constitutions, on accident and force." (No. 1)

For those convinced that America's salvation turned on the creation of a truly federal union, featuring a sufficiently empowered central government, the Framers had vindicated the cause of republicanism; they had "saved the revolution." Of course, it was still up to "the people," that is, the state ratifying conventions, to embrace the remedy. In New York, a state whose adoption of the Constitution would be crucial to the success of the new government, there were signs of strong opposition to the "cure." It was this critical episode in the ratification contest that gave rise to *The Federalist*. Given its authors' belief that the fate of the American nation (and the cause of republicanism itself) hung in the balance, they spared no sensible argument that might be made on behalf of ratification. This included heralding the virtues of a "new-and-improved" federal republic, as well as underscoring, in the starkest terms, the dire consequences of rejecting the plan. There can be little doubt that the latter was intended to "scare hell out of the American people,"[35] or at least the citizens of New York. This is not to suggest that Publius was guilty of "alarmism," for the sense of crisis in 1787 was palpable, and his fearful predictions for the rudderless nation were well within the realm of probability.[36] It does, however, suggest a conscious rhetorical strategy designed to impress upon his readers the necessity of adopting the proposed plan of union. In short, Publius had to neutralize the fear of an oppressive central authority—the Constitution did, after all, reverse the essential relationship between state and national governments—with the more potent specters of secession, separate confederacies, civil war, foreign intrigue, and even conquest.[37] As the following passage illustrates, Madison's prose was up to the task:

> The picture of the consequences of disunion cannot be too highly colored, or too often exhibited. Every man who loves, peace, every man who loves his country, every man who loves liberty, ought to have it before his eyes, that he may cherish in his heart a due attachment to the Union of America, and be able to set a due value on the means of preserving it. (No. 41)

Under the circumstances, persuading Americans that the general government required expanded powers and greater "energy" was a relatively easy task. The new nation was quickly learning a simple but profound political truth: that weak and lethargic government is not the same as good government, nor strong and energetic government necessarily oppressive.[38] Evidence of this maxim was all too apparent when the call went out to the states for holding a federal convention. The great difficulty Publius faced was defending a species of "republican" government that (at the national level) *pushed the concepts of popular representation and majority rule to the vanishing point*. In doing so, his knowledge of history (and the example of the state legislatures under the Confederation) proved indispensable, for it informed him that popular majorities could be just as arbitrary as monarchs, and demagogues as dangerous to liberty as despots.[39] This was another of those simple truths "suggested by reason, illustrated by [historical] examples, and enforced by our own experience" (No. 63) that proved critical in the deliberations of the Federal Convention. Its corollary, that one "must first enable the government to control the governed: and in the next place, oblige it to control itself" (No. 51), suggested that the patently "undemocratic" features of the Constitution were actually essential safeguards for the survival of an *American* polity.

Though used to great effect, Publius does not rely solely on historical precedent or America's recent past to support his various conclusions, but frequently invokes something even more universal to reinforce the need for "auxiliary precautions"—*human nature*. Man's nature, Hamilton observes, makes government necessary in the first place; for "the passions of men will not conform to the dictates of reason and justice, without constraint." (No. 15) Like Plato, Publius identifies reason with justice, and views passion and prejudice as the enemies of both. Yet unlike Plato, he is willing to meet men's "pride and prejudice" on their own terms, and even turns them to the ends of republicanism. This notion, that the prevalence of self-interested behavior is compatible with republican government, that widespread "civic virtue" (in the classical sense) is not essential for its viability, was one of the most startling political revelations to appear since the Renaissance.[40]

The conspicuous presence of the "self-interested" and "passionate" man in *The Federalist* may be credited to the authors' experience and research, but more importantly it serves a theoretical, and ultimately, a rhetorical function. Publius faced a predicament similar to John Locke's, once the latter adopted the natural rights philosophy of Hobbes as a starting point for his own theory of *limited* government. Locke agreed that men were by nature free, equal, sovereign and self-interested, but denied Hobbes' claim that they were so prone to contentiousness that their very survival depended on renouncing their "natural rights" (except self-preservation), and transferring their "sovereignty" to an absolute ruler. On the other hand, Locke had to show that at least *some* men were nearer to the brutes than the angels in order to justify the forfeiture of "natural liberty" for the "constraints" of civil society.[41] At a more refined, but no less crucial level, Publius had to defend highly indirect forms of representation and "undemocratic" constitutional mechanisms, while showing that the people remained "sovereign" and continued to "govern" themselves. As with history and reason, human nature is put to a number of uses in *The Federalist*, but nowhere more ingeniously than in resolving this paradox.

It has been observed that the rather stark picture of human nature presented in *The Federalist* signaled a final abandonment of the "civic virtue" tradition of classical republican thought.[42] In America the emphasis on civic virtue as the touchstone of republicanism peaked in the days between the imposition of the "Intolerable Acts" in 1774 and the military setbacks of late 1776. The experience of the war and the first years of independence convinced many that men in America, high and low, were not immune to the foibles and vices that characterized the rest of mankind. Americans were unique, and undeniably possessed a "genius" for self-government; yet in all too many cases they had exhibited a selfish disregard for the public good. Madison, Hamilton, and Jay recognized sooner than most that a republican society (particularly a modern, commercial one) could not be sustained on the basis of the assumed good-will and voluntary cooperation of its members. The American republic, they concluded, could not live on virtue alone.[43] It was high time, there-fore, to awaken from this "deceitful dream of a golden age," and to take "as a practical maxim for the direction of our political conduct, that we, as well as the other inhabitants of the globe, are yet remote from the happy empire of perfect wisdom and perfect virtue." (No. 7)

This frank admission of mankind's imperfection and fallibility (in-cluding *homo Americanus*) represents the decisive turning point in American political and constitutional history.[44] It not only set the stage for reversing the relationship between the states and the general govern-ment, but justified denying the people a means of translating their collective "will" into national policy. This second modification was achieved through indirect modes of representation and an intricate array of constitutional checks. Defending these "undemocratic" features of an ostensibly "popular" government tested the outer limits of political wis-dom. Only a monitory reading of history and a candid consideration of human nature, Publius suggests, can provide a convincing rationale. The latter centers on the notion that the "errors and prejudice" of men may co-exist with their "good sense and wisdom." (No. 85) To one degree or another, all societies, no less than all men, exhibit signs of both. "The supposition of universal venality in human nature," Hamilton writes, "is little less an error in political reasoning than the supposition of universal rectitude." (No. 76)[45] Accordingly, man's capacity for goodness, no less than his propensity for "mischief," must figure into any scheme of gov-ernment that aims to simultaneously maintain order and preserve liberty.[46] Publius' commitment to "popular" government implies a belief that the good in man outweighs the bad, and he freely admits that "Republican government presupposes the existence of [virtuous] qualities in a higher degree than any other form." (No. 55) Yet despite such reassurances—and the expressed intent of taking "human nature as it is, without flattering its virtues or exaggerating its vices" (No. 76)—the emphasis in *The Fed-eralist* falls roundly on the darker side.

It appears ironic that men like Hamilton, Madison, and Jay, who so often exemplified reason and virtue in public life, were willing to toler-ate their opposites in the body politic. Indeed, it seems rather odd that the same men who consistently denounced the passions and prejudices of mankind should recommend a government that not only acknowl-edged the pervasiveness of these "defects," but openly aimed to accommodate them?[47] The irony and oddity fade, however, when we con-sider the task faced by the Constitution's defenders. Without joining Plato and speaking the unspeakable (that the mass of men are more creatures of "errors and prejudice" than of "good sense and wisdom"), they had to resolve the paradox of an "undemocratic" democracy. They had to justify a "popular" government that deliberately prohibited the people from governing at the national level.[48] Publius knew that he and many of his peers were reasonable and informed, but he did not annex these qualities to the common stock of humanity. As Madison confided to Edmund Randolph in the midst of the ratification contest, "there can be no doubt that there are subjects to which the capacities of the bulk of mankind are unequal, and on which they must and will be governed by those with whom they happen to have acquaintance and confidence."[49] With this sentiment, Hamilton, well-known for his poor opinion of the "unreflecting multitude," was in full agreement.[50]

Such "elitist" confessions are a key to understanding the theory of representation in *The Federalist*. Practical considerations aside, the unequal distribution of knowledge, reasonableness, and virtue suggested that the populace could not be relied upon to govern responsibly over the long run. On the other hand, it was necessary to assume, even stress, that in spite of these discrepancies, the "bulk of mankind" was discriminating enough to select those who could.[51] The experience of America, particularly as measured by the high standards of the Revolutionary leadership, generally confirmed the assertion. At the crossroads of judgment and policy, the majority of men were perhaps inept, but they could be safely entrusted with directly electing *some* of their national representatives.[52]

A system of indirect representation through which the voice of the people might be "filtered" and "refined" was, however, only part of the solution. This would "enable the government to [better] control the governed," but it was just as necessary to "oblige it to control itself." Faction, Publius reminds his readers, has two faces, a popular one and a governmental one; one acts from below, the other from above. By the mid-1780s, the behavior of the states had convinced many that the main threat from above was an unchecked "tyrannical" legislature.[53] This led the Framers away from the doctrine of "legislative supremacy" (central to the first state constitutions), and toward the tenets of blended powers and checks and balances. Sharp divisions were still expected in the national legislature, for if "men of equal integrity and discernment" often find themselves at odds, the added factors of pride, ambition, and "clashing interests" make factions all the more inevitable.[54] Yet by partitioning and checking legislative power, the "pestilential breath of faction" (No. 81) could be substantially diffused.

Publius' concern with "controlling" government reveals an additional aspect of his political psychology, and one which cuts across his distinction between the "unthinking many" and the "reasoning few." For if "the people" collectively cannot be entrusted with power, neither can those to whom it is granted be expected to use it honestly or wisely. "Enlightened statesmen," Madison observes, "will not always be at the helm." (No. 10) It is this view—that defects of judgment and motive will at one time or another infect the councils of government—which distances Publius from that species of elitism which would glibly entrust political power to society's "betters."[55] Public officials, no less than the people themselves, must be limited, checked, and restrained. Moreover, structural factors, such as the size of a legislative body, are no less vital to good government than the qualities of the members themselves. "Had every Athenian been a Socrates," Madison wryly observes, "every Athenian assembly would still have been a mob." (No. 55)

Here and elsewhere Publius notes that the viability of a republican regime does not exclusively turn on the classical polarities of the informed vs. the ignorant, the rational vs. the passionate, or the selfish vs. the disinterested. These terms still carried meaning, but they were no longer applied in their "classical," much less Platonic sense.[56] True, the people must be limited in their capacity to influence the national councils; but so too must the "counsellors." The first may be achieved via indirect modes of representation; the second by a combination of bicameralism, executive veto, super-majorities, life tenure for judges, and judicial review—in short, checks and balances. Working in conjunction, these "auxiliary precautions" would regulate and control the ultimate bane of popular government and the gravest threat to both individual rights and the social order: unchecked *factions*, the "latent causes" of which are "sown in the nature of man." (No. 10)

# *Conclusion*

THE PRINCIPAL AIM of this essay has been to identify the methodological foundations of *The Federalist*, and to suggest how these inform the judgments and reveal the aims of "Publius." As we have seen, the "science" of *The Federalist* centers on the prudent application of reason, the relevant past, and a knowledge of human nature to the task of establishing (and explicating) the fundamental law for a just and enduring polity. In America this resulted in adopting the framework of an *extended republic*, constituted along both *national* and *(con)federal* lines, and assuming a *mixed* (democratic, oligarchic, and monarchical) form.

This method, as applied by the Framers, was indispensable to the ultimate success of the Constitution and to the longevity of popular government in the United States. That Publius was consciously aware of this fact is implicit in many of the papers. Yet in the following passage, Madison makes a direct and exalted reference to the Framers' (and his own) approach to the science of government:

> Is it not the glory of the people of America, that whilst they have paid a decent regard to the opinions of former times and other nations, they have not suffered a blind veneration for antiquity, for custom, or for names, to overrule suggestions of their own good sense, the knowledge of their own situation, and the lessons of their own experience? (No. 14)

Knowledge, good sense, experience—these few words, like no others, capture the essence of the Framers' method and the *science of Publius*. By consistently adhering to these guiding principles of statecraft, the men who gathered in Philadelphia were able to hammer out a frame of government that might fulfill the broader promise of republican *society*. Madison, Hamilton, and Jay, the unsurpassed expositors of the Framers' creation, achieved a parallel success in the realm of political theory. In Francis Bacon's felicitous phrase, they consummated "a true and lawful marriage between the empirical and rational faculty." The reference to Bacon is apt, for *The Federalist*, unlike most excursions into political theory, is truly fruitful in "works." As one admirer has written, "[*The Federalist*] is a theoretical undertaking whose benefits may extend to the most distant posterity, indeed to anyone, any time, who has the necessary diligence and intelligence to devote to Publius's handiwork."[57]

## NOTES

1. Peter Gay, *The Enlightenment: The Science of Freedom* (New York, 1969), 3–12.

2. Descartes' *Meditations* (1641), Hobbes' *Leviathan* (1651) and Spinoza's *Ethics* (1677) are classics of this genre.

3. The following generalizations on the *philosophes* are just that, generalizations. All broadly-based intellectual movements are invariably marked by diversity and dissent, and the Enlightenment was rich in both. The aim here is to highlight a few characteristic features of the period that are relevant to my subject. A series of qualifications, however judicious, would have served little purpose. For illuminating discussions of Enlightenment views on subjects only touched on here, see Peter Gay, *The Enlightenment: An Interpretation*, 2 vols. (New York, 1966, 1969); Paul Hazard, *European Thought in the Eighteenth Century* (Cleveland, 1963); and Ernst

Cassirer, *The Philosophy of the Enlightenment*, trans. Fritz C. A. Koelin and James Pettegrove (Boston, 1955). For a good introduction to the period, see Norman Hampson, *The Enlightenment* (New York, 1968).

4. Henry Steele Commager, *Jefferson, Nationalism, and the Enlightenment* (New York, 1975), 3. Commager's *Jefferson* is an inspired and accessible account of the American Enlightenment and the achievement of the Founders. More detailed and scholarly is Commager's *The Empire of Reason: How Europe Imagined and America Realized The Enlightenment* (Garden City, N.Y., 1977). See also Henry F. May, *The Enlightenment in America* (New York, 1976).

5. Though written before the adoption of the Constitution, George Washington's famous "Circular Letter" (June, 1783) is unsurpassed as an expression of the triumphant spirit of the American Enlightenment. "The foundation of our Empire," Washington relates, "was not laid in the gloomy age of Ignorance and Superstition, but at an Epocha when the rights of mankind were better understood and more clearly defined, than at any former period; the researches of the human mind after social happiness, have been carried to a great extent, the treasures of knowledge, acquired by the labours of Philosophers, Sages, and Legislators, through a long succession of years are laid open for our use, and their collective wisdom, may be happily applied in the Establishment of our forms of Government." Quoted in Gay, *Science of Freedom*, 560. Echoing Washington's sentiments, Noah Webster declared that the work of the Framers had splendidly confirmed that the American republic was indeed *"an empire of reason."* "An Examination into the Leading Principles of the Federal Constitution," October 1787, Paul L. Ford, ed., *Pamphlets on the Constitution of the United States* (Boston, 1888), 29.

6. Donald Meyer, for example, notes that *"The Federalist* would seem to bear out Hannah Arendt's claim that the American Revolution produced no political science, and that the Constitution-makers were informed more by 'experience' than by reason or theory." *The Democratic Enlightenment* (New York, 1976), 155–56.

7. Much has been written on *The Federalist*, particularly in more recent years. Full-length studies include, Gottfried Dietz, *The Federalist: A Classic on Federalism and Free Government* (Baltimore, 1960); Garry Wills, *Explaining America: The Federalist* (New York, 1981); David F. Epstein, *The Political Theory of The Federalist* (Chicago, 1984); Albert Furtwangler, *The Authority of Publius: A Reading of The Federalist Papers* (Ithaca, N.Y., 1984); Morton White, *Philosophy, The Federalist, and the Constitution* (New York, 1987); Edward Millican, *One United People: The Federalist Papers and the National Idea* (Lexington, Ky., 1990); and George W. Carey, *The Federalist: Design for a Constitutional Republic* (Urbana, Ill., 1989). While I have consulted these and other sources, the focus and findings presented here owe more to an intimacy with *The Federalist* than to an immersion in the secondary literature.

8. For a superb account of the "making" (and meaning) of *The Federalist*, see Richard B. Morris, *Witnesses at the Creation: Hamilton, Madison, Jay and the Constitution* (New York, 1987).

9. As Madison notes in *Federalist* No. 37, "the ultimate object of these papers is to determine clearly and fully the merits of this Constitution, and the expediency of adopting it."

10. A notable exception is Leo Strauss and Joseph Cropsey, eds., *The History of Political Philosophy*, 3rd ed. (Chicago, 1987), which includes Martin Diamond's "The Federalist," 659–79.

11. In addition to this "deficiency," it is sometimes suggested that *The Federalist* is also deficient in logic, psychology, and historiography. Given the numerous merits of the work, this is rarely presented as a serious detraction. In general, I agree with Commager's assessment that despite the "limits" of the Framers' knowledge,

"somehow it worked rather better" than our own. *Jefferson*, xiv. In a similar vein, Neal Riemer notes that "[t]he sophisticated philosopher, the modern psychologist, and the empirical political theorist may throw up his hands in disgust at Madison's abstractions, methods, and axioms. The statesman, however, will find in Madison insights of prescriptive validity." *James Madison: Creating the Constitution* (Washington, D. C., 1986), 34.

12. Though not without intelligent detractors (e.g., Robert Dahl), *The Federalist* is among the most widely admired works of political science. Thomas Jefferson, who had no hand in the drafting or ratification of the Constitution, called it "the best commentary on the principles of government which was ever written." George Washington correctly predicted that it would "merit the notice of posterity." Even Charles Beard, famous for his "economic" interpretation of the Constitution, called *The Federalist* "the most instructive work on political science ever written in the United States; and, owing to its practical character, it ranks first in the world's literature of political science." *The Enduring Federalist* (New York, 1948), 10. More recently, Peter Gay has paid homage by crowning his landmark study of the Enlightenment with a tribute to *The Federalist*. Its authors, Gay writes, "sound all the great themes of the Enlightenment, if by implication only: the dialectical movement away from Christianity to modernity; the pessimistic though wholly secular appraisal of human nature coupled with an optimistic confidence in instrumental arrangements; the pragmatic reading of history as an aid to political sociology; the humane philosophy underlying their plea for the proposed constitution; the commitment to the critical method and the eloquent advocacy of practicality." The work of Publius, Gay concludes, "fully deserves immortality as a classic in the art of politics." *Science of Freedom*, 563.

13. Emphasis added. *The Debates in the Several State Conventions on the Adoption of the Federal Convention* . . . ed., Jonathan Elliot, 5 vols., 2nd ed. (Philadelphia, 1876), II:301.

14. "In the whole political literature," Commager asks, "is there a more reasonable document than *The Federalist*?" *Jefferson*, xiv.

15. The notion that Americans had, in a single decade, greatly advanced the "science of politics" was a common belief of the time. For example, Edmund Randolph of Virginia reminded his colleagues at the Federal Convention that the framers of the Articles of Confederation could not be blamed for its inadequacies, given "the then infancy of the science, of constitutions, & of confederacies." Max Farrand, ed., *The Records of the Federal Convention of 1787*, 4 vols. (New Haven, 1966), I:18. In the interim, however, Americans had made "valuable improvements . . . on the popular models" of government; advances which "cannot certainly be too much admired." (No. 10)

16. As Garry Wills observes, Publius "is aspiring to the Enlightenment's supreme goal, the construction of a science of man to rank with the Newtonian science of inanimate nature." *Explaining America*, 91. In the opinion of David Ramsay, member of the Confederation Congress and delegate to the South Carolina ratifying convention, the Framers had placed "the science of politics on a footing with the other sciences, by opening it to improvements from experience, and the discoveries of future ages." Quoted in Gordon S. Wood, *The Creation of the American Republic, 1776–1787* (New York, 1969), 613. On the influence of "hard" science on the Founders, see I. Bernard Cohen, *Science and the Founding Fathers: Science in the Political Thought of Thomas Jefferson, Benjamin Franklin, John Adams, and James Madison* (New York, 1995).

17. In this belief, which so influenced their political thinking, Hamilton and Madison were deeply indebted to the writers of the Scottish Enlightenment, par-

ticularly David Hume. See Douglas G. Adair, "'That Politics May Be Reduced to a Science': David Hume, James Madison and the Tenth *Federalist*," *The Huntington Library Quarterly* 20 (1957), 343–60; Roy Branson, "James Madison and the Scottish Enlightenment," *Journal of the History of Ideas* 40 (1979) 235–50; Theodore Draper, "Hume and Madison: The Secrets of Federalist Paper No. 10," *Encounter* 58 (1982), 34–47; and Wills, *Explaining America, passim.*

18. Elsewhere Hamilton defines a self-evident truth as "one . . . which to a correct and unprejudiced mind, carries its own evidence with it; and may be obscured, but cannot be made plainer by argument or reasoning." (No. 23)

19. During the ratification contest, Madison observed that "[t]he diversity of opinions . . . among men of equal integrity & discernment, is at once a melancholy proof of the fallibility of the human judgment, and of the imperfect progress yet made in the science of Government." To Archibald Stuart, October 30, 1787, *The Papers of James Madison*, eds., Robert A. Rutland et al. (Chicago, 1977), X: 232. John Jay similarly concluded that "on a subject so comprehensive, and involving such a variety of points and questions, the most able, the most candid, and the most honest men will differ in opinion." "An Address to the People of the State of New York," April 1788, Ford, *Pamphlets*, 79.

20. August 13, 1787, Farrand, *Records*, II:278. See Douglas Adair, "'Experience Must Be Our Only Guide': History, Democratic Theory, and the United States Constitution," in Trevor Colbourn, ed., *Fame and the Founding Fathers: Essays by Douglas Adair* (New York, 1974), 107–23.

21. What has been said of Madison may be applied to Publius: "he understood well that theory, abstractly and dogmatically conceived, is unreal and can be mischievous. He insisted that certain 'pure' theories were erroneous or dangerous." Riemer, *Madison*, 13. Jay was equally emphatic in declaring that "experience will better determine . . . [political] questions than theoretical arguments." "Address," Ford, *Pamphlets*, 85.

22. Hamilton (quoted here), like Madison and Jay, had little more than contempt for "closet" political theorists, American or otherwise. In a letter to Marquis de Lafayette at the outset of the French Revolution, Hamilton issued a prophetic warning on the dangers of abstract political theory: "I dread the reveries of your Philosophic politicians who appear in the moment to have great influence and who being mere speculatists may aim at more refinement than suits either with human nature or the composition of your nation." To Lafayette, October 6, 1789, *The Papers of Alexander Hamilton*, ed., Harold C. Syrett (27 vols., New York, 1961–1987), V:425.

23. While Madison's long political career was full of shifts and turns, he never modified his opinion that "theories are the offspring of the closet; expectations and qualifications the lessons of experience." To Charles J. Ingersoll (1835); quoted in Riemer, *Madison*, 13. Over the course of a long career, this attitude gave Madison the flexibility to adjust to changed circumstances, while remaining faithful to his republican principles.

24. In 1787 many observers believed that America's political demise would be catastrophic to the cause of liberty and self-government. "[A] wrong election on the part we shall act," Publius warned, "may . . . deserve to be considered as the general misfortune of mankind." (No. 1) Elsewhere (and with chilling brevity), Madison writes, "The moment of [the Union's] dissolution, will be a new order of things." (No. 41) Similarly, Hamilton declared in the Federal Convention, that "if we did not give to that form [republicanism] due stability and wisdom, it would be disgraced & lost among ourselves, and disgraced & lost to mankind forever." Farrand, *Records*, I:424. In a passage of stark eloquence, Jay provided the basis for this fear. "Let us also be mindful

that the cause of freedom greatly depends on the use we make of the singular opportunities we enjoy of governing ourselves wisely; for if the event should prove, that the
people of this country either cannot or will not govern themselves, who will hereafter
be advocates for systems, which, however charming in theory and prospect, are not
reducible to practice. If the people of our nation, instead of consenting to be governed
by laws of their own making and rulers of their own choosing, should let licentiousness, disorder, and confusion reign over them, the minds of men every where, will
insensibly become alienated from republican forms, and prepared to prefer and acquiesce in Governments, which, though less friendly to liberty, afford more peace and
security." "Address," Ford, *Pamphlets*, 86.

25. In his "Letters of Fabius," written in support of the Constitution, John
Dickinson noted that "History is entertaining and instructive; but if admired chiefly
for amusement, it may yield little profit." Ford, *Pamphlets*, 189. This view of the
"uses" of history prevailed among the Founding generation.

26. Like Jay (quoted here), Madison looked to history for prescriptive truths.
In his study, "Of Ancient and Modern Confederacies," Madison echoed French
*philosophe* Charles Pinot Duclos in observing that "the past should enlighten us on
the future: knowledge of history is no more than anticipated experience . . . Where
we see the same faults followed regularly by the same misfortunes, we may reasonably think that if we could have known the first we might have avoided the others."
Rutland, *Madison*, vol. 9: 3.

27. A deliberately cautious use of history in *The Federalist* is evident in a number of instances. For example, Madison informs his readers, "I am not unaware of
the circumstances which distinguish the American from other forms of popular governments, as well ancient and modern; and which render extreme circumspection
necessary in reasoning from the one case to the other." (No. 63) In general, Publius
deems historical inference relevant only "[s]o far as [the] case will admit of comparison with that of the United States." (No. 19)

28. "The great theater of the United States," Publius observes, "presents a
very different scene" (No. 53), and "[t]he novelty of the undertaking immediately
strikes us." (No. 37) Madison, who made a thorough study of leagues and confederacies in preparation for the Federal Convention, noted its limited use in
constructing a new government. As all past systems had failed, they could "furnish
no other light than that of beacons, which give warning of the course to be shunned,
without pointing out that which ought to be pursued." (No. 37) Any "errors" in the
proposed Constitution, therefore, were not attributable to "a want of accuracy or
care in the investigation," but "rather from the defect of antecedent experience on
this complicated and difficult subject." (No. 38) For the Founders' views on the
political implications of American "exceptionalism," see Peter Hoffer, *Revolution
and Regeneration: Life Cycles and the Historical Vision of the Generation of 1776* (Athens,
Ga., 1983), 11–69. For a more direct discussion of "The Founders' Interpretive
Uses of History," see David A. J. Richards, *Foundations of American Constitutionalism*
(New York, 1989), 19–77.

29. John Jay, in recommending the Constitution to his fellow New Yorkers,
observed that "[e]xperience is a severe preceptor, but it teaches useful truths, and
however harsh, is always honest—Be calm and dispassionate, and listen to what it
tells us." "Address," Ford, *Pamphlets*, 71.

30. The role of human nature in *The Federalist* has been examined in a num-
ber of contexts. In addition to the full-length studies cited above, see Benjamin F.
Wright, "*The Federalist* on the Nature of Political Man," *Ethics* 59 (1949), 1–31;
James P. Scanlan, "*The Federalist* and Human Nature," *Review of Politics* 21 (1959),
657–77; Maynard Smith, "Reason, Passion and Political Freedom in *The Federalist*,"
*Journal of Politics* 22 (1960), 535–44; Joseph F. Kobylka and Bradley Kent Carter,

"Madison, *The Federalist*, and the Constitutional Order: Human Nature and Institutional Structure," *Polity* 20 (1987), 190–208; Daniel W. Howe, "The Political Psychology of *The Federalist*," *William and Mary Quarterly* 44 (1987), 485–509; and Arthur O. Lovejoy, "The Theory of Human Nature in the American Constitution," in *Reflections on Human Nature* (Baltimore, 1961), 37–65.

31. In the Federal Convention Hamilton asserted that "The science of policy is the knowledge of human nature." Farrand, *Records*, I:378. A year later, at Poughkeepsie, Hamilton confirmed that "[t]here are certain social principles in human nature, from which we may draw the most solid conclusions with respect to the conduct of individuals and of communities." Elliot, *Debates*, III:354. For this reason, as John Jay inferred, it was absolutely essential that the American systems of government be "adapted on the actual state of human nature." To Jefferson, April 24, 1787, *The Correspondence and Public Papers of John Jay*, ed., Henry P. Johnston, 4 vols. (New York, 1890–1893), III:245.

32. A handful of passing references to "natural rights," the "law of nature," the "state of nature," and the "social compact" appear in *The Federalist*, but are not elaborated upon. Given the near universal acceptance of natural rights philosophy and the compact theory of government among his countrymen, Publius had little need to argue (or even establish) their validity. As such, these function as articles of republican faith; the first being "self-evident," the second, a "direct inference" from the first.

33. Madison to Thomas Jefferson, March 19, 1787, Rutland, *Madison*, IX: 318.

34. Quoted in Wood, *American Republic*, 472. At the same time Jay informed Jefferson that "there is reason to fear that too much has been expected from the virtue and good sense of the people." To Jefferson, February 9, 1787, *Correspondence*, III:232.

35. Those familiar with the origins of the Cold War will recognize the words of Senator Arthur Vandenburg, who informed President Truman in 1947 that it would be necessary to frighten Congress in order to obtain support for anti-communist efforts in Greece and Turkey. In a more eloquent, but no less determined manner, Publius also adopted this method of persuasion.

36. With the notable exception of Thomas Jefferson, who was serving as minister to France at the time, the correspondence of many of America's leading (and lesser) voices was filled with a grave sense of crisis. Washington's remarks are indicative: "the situation of the General Government (if it can be called a government) is shaken to its foundation and liable to be overset by every blast. In a word, it is at an end, and unless a remedy is soon applied, anarchy and confusion will inevitably ensue." To Jefferson, May 30, 1787, Julian P. Boyd, ed., *The Papers of Thomas Jefferson* (Princeton, 1955), XI: 389–90. As Gordon Wood notes, "By the mid-eighties the oratory and writings were filled with talk of crisis to the point of redundancy." *American Republic*, 393.

37. The fact that key advocates of a strengthened national authority shared a "Continental" outlook and were strongly influenced by international considerations should not be overlooked when considering the motives of the Framers. The authors of *The Federalist*, along with Washington, were arguably the most significant among the continentally-minded nationalists. See Gerald Stourzh, *Alexander Hamilton and the Idea of Republican Government* (Stanford, 1970), 126–205; and Stanley Elkins and Eric McKitrick, "The Founding Fathers: Young Men of the Revolution," *Political Science Quarterly*, 76 (1961), 181–216.

38. Madison and Hamilton were in the vanguard of those demanding expanded powers for the general government. As early as 1780, Madison recommended legislation in Congress which aimed to bolster the national authority. Hamilton's recognition of the "defects of our present system," dates from the same time. In a

letter to James Duane, a New York delegate to Congress, Hamilton diagnosed the fatal ills of the general government and urgently called for a constitutional convention ("the sooner, the better") to strengthen its powers. To Duane, September 3, 1780, Syrett, *Hamilton*, II: 400, 407. This "Liberty Pole" letter, which possibly circulated among nationalists in Congress, was "the first clear-cut, responsible appeal for the kind of convention that met at last in 1787." Clinton Rossiter, *Alexander Hamilton and the Constitution* (New York, 1964), 36–37.

39. The concept of the "tyranny of the majority" and the likely prospect that the unbridled rule of the *demos* would end in despotism was first developed by Plato in *The Republic*. Like the Greek philosopher, Publius opposed majoritarian democracy on both philosophical and practical grounds. "[N]o maxim . . . is more liable to be misapplied," Madison observed, "than the current one that the interest of the majority is the political standard of right and wrong." To James Monroe, October 5, 1786, Rutland, *Madison*, IX: 141. As for practical concerns, Madison (drawing heavily on Hume) found a "solution" to those "diseases most incident to Republican Government" (No. 10) in the concept of an "extended republic" composed of a "multiplicity of interests." (No. 51) Douglas Adair has called Madison's solution, "the greatest triumph in the practical application of the Enlightenment ideal of scientific political research." "James Madison," in Colbourne, *Fame*, 135. See also George W. Carey, "Majority Tyranny and the Extended Republic Theory of James Madison," *Modern Age* 20 (1976), 40–53.

40. Here and elsewhere the American Founders were anticipated by the republican writings of Niccolò Machiavelli (1469–1527). For a systematic comparison, see Quentin P. Taylor, "Machiavelli and the American Republic," in *The Other Machiavelli: Republican Writings by the Author of the "Prince"* (Lanham, Md., 1998), 1–42.

41. C. B. Macpherson, "The Social Bearing of Locke's Political Theory," *Western Political Quarterly* 8 (1954), 1–22. For an interesting comparative study, see George Mace, *Locke, Hobbes, and The Federalist Papers* (Carbondale, Ill., 1979).

42. The transition in American political thought from "classical republicanism" (rooted in civic virtue) to "liberal democracy" (rooted in self–interest) is a central theme in the scholarship on "the critical period." Much of the discussion (which has spawned an enormous literature) was sparked by Gordon Wood's influential *Creation of the American Republic*.

43. In the words of Herbert Storing, the alternative for Publius was to rest "his argument for the primacy of the Union, not on any notion of a band of brothers or popular patriotism and self-restraint, but on self-interest and private passion, properly regulated." "The Federal Convention of 1787," in Ralph A. Rossum and Gary L. McDowell, eds., *The American Founding* (Washington, D.C., 1981), 22.

44. As Hamilton writes, the belief that "a sense of common interest would preside over the conduct" of the states, "and would beget a full compliance with all the constitutional requisitions" under the Articles, "betrayed an ignorance of the true springs by which human conduct is actuated." (No. 15)

45. As Rossum and McDowell observe, the Framers "were required to plumb the depths of human nature, to take account of both its virtues and its vices, to accommodate political theory to the 'genius of the people,' and to fashion institutional arrangements to supply the defect of better motives." "Politics, Statesmanship, and the Constitution," in *American Founding*, 10–11.

46. Elsewhere Hamilton writes, "No plan of governing is well founded, which does not regard man as a compound of selfish and virtuous passions. To expect him to be wholly guided by the latter, would be as great an error as to suppose him wholly destitute of them." "Draft of President Washington's Address to Congress,"

December 7, 1796, in Richard B. Morris, ed., *Alexander Hamilton and the Founding of the Nation* (New York, 1957), 144.

47. This does not mean that Publius envisaged an "invisible hand" theory of pluralism or ascribed to the notion that "private vice, makes public virtue." Madison in particular, underscored the distinction between the transient and partial interests of society, and "the permanent and aggregate interests of the community." (No. 10) Moreover, the very preference for a representative republic presupposed an adequate degree of civic-mindedness and political competence among the people and their leaders. (No. 55) Nevertheless, in some cases, individual egoism, no less than higher motives, works to the advantage of the "public good." Madison, for instance, observes that the ties between a representative and his constituents "are strengthened by motives of a more selfish nature. His pride and vanity attach him to a form of government and gives him a share in its honors and distinctions." (No. 57)

48. That Madison in particular viewed this difficulty as a "paradox" is suggested by his remark in the Convention that an extended republic "was the only defense against the inconveniences of democracy consistent with the democratic form of Government." Farrand, *Records*, I:134–35. This "defense" formed the basis of Publius' distinction between a pure "democracy," like ancient Athens, and a representative "republic," like the United States. The latter, Madison writes, involves *"the total exclusion of the people in their collective capacity* from any share in [the national government]." (No. 63)

49. Madison to Edmund Randolph, January 10, 1788, Rutland, *Madison*, X: 355.

50. In the second number of his "Caesar" letters (thought to have been written by Hamilton shortly before the invention of Publius), the author bluntly asserts, "the mass of the people of America (any more than the mass of other countries) cannot judge with any degree of precision concerning the fitness of this New Constitution to the peculiar situation of America." John P. Kaminski and Gaspare J. Saladino, eds., *Commentaries on the Constitution . . .* , vol. 13 of *The Documentary History of the Ratification of the Constitution* (Madison, Wis., 1981), 397.

51. As Madison stated on June 20, 1788, in the Virginia ratifying convention, a commitment to republicanism implied a belief that the common people possessed sufficient "virtue and intelligence to select men of virtue and wisdom." Moreover, if this belief were misplaced, "[n]o theoretical checks, no form of government, can render us secure." Elliot, *Debates*, III:536–37. As suggested above, the existence of a broad-based republican *ethos* was a necessary presupposition among the Framers.

52. Under the proposed Constitution, members of the House of Representatives were the only national officials chosen by "the people" directly, which in 1788 meant adult white males, who either owned property or paid taxes.

53. As physician-statesman Benjamin Rush observed, "In our opposition to monarchy, we forgot that the temple of tyranny has two doors. We bolted one of them by proper restraints; but we left the other open, by neglecting to guard against the effects of our own ignorance and licentiousness." "Address," (1787), *Principles and Acts of the Revolution in America*, ed., Hezekiah Niles (New York, 1876), 234. Similarly, James Wilson informed his fellow delegates in Philadelphia that "[d]espotism comes on mankind in different shapes: sometimes in an Executive, sometimes in a military one. Is there no danger of a Legislative despotism? Theory & practice both proclaim it." Farrand, *Records*, I:254.

54. In an insightful and high-minded passage, Hamilton writes: "So numerous indeed and so powerful are the causes which serve to give a false bias to the judgment, that we upon many occasions, see wise and good men on the wrong as well as the right side of questions, of the first magnitude to society. This circumstance, if duly attended

to, would furnish a lesson of moderation to those, who are ever so much persuaded of their caution, in this respect, might be drawn from reflection, that we are not always sure, that those who advocate the truth are influenced by purer principles than their antagonists. Ambition, avarice, personal animosity, party opposition, and many other motives, not more laudable than these, are apt to operate as well upon those who support as upon those who oppose the right side of a question." (No. 1)

55. For this reason I have resisted the temptation to apply C. B. Macpherson's notion of "differential rationality" of social classes to Publius. See *The Political Theory of Possessive Individualism: Hobbes to Locke* (New York, 1962), 221–38. As noted above, Publius does make distinctions among the populace, but these are based more on individual differences of character, judgment, and talent than on economic status. Conversely, he applies the former criteria in making distinctions *within* social classes. As Hamilton told the Poughkeepsie ratifying convention, "Experience has by no means justified us in the supposition that there is more virtue in one class of men than in another." Elliot, *Debates*, II:257. In a different context, Hamilton would note the troubling implications of "talents without wealth," "talents without virtue," and the "wealthy but incapable." "Draft," Morris, *Hamilton*, 144. By this he did not mean that social class was irrelevant to leadership, for on the whole "the advantage of character belongs to the wealthy." Similarly, Hamilton notes that both rich and poor are characterized by "vices," but those of the rich "are probably more favorable to the prosperity of the state than those of the indigent." Elliot, *Debates*, II:257. A clear statement of the political implications of social class appears in *The Federalist*, where Hamilton notes that "from the natural operation of the different interests and views of the various classes of the community," the people's representatives "will consist almost entirely of proprietors of land, of merchants and members of the learned professions, who will truly represent all those different interests and views." (No. 36) This synthesis of class interest and representation is crowned by a commitment to meritocracy. As Hamilton observes, the experience of America had unequivocally shown that "[t]here are strong minds in every walk of life that will rise superior to the disadvantages of situation." As a general principle, then, "The door ought to be equally open to all." (No. 36) These judicious qualifications must frustrate all attempts to apply such labels as "elitist" or "egalitarian," "oligarchic" or "democratic" to the Framers' intentions or to the Constitution itself.

56. A more fascinating political conversation can hardly be conjured than one between Plato circa *The Republic*, and Madison and Hamilton circa *The Federalist*. I sense there would be more points of agreement than immediately suggest themselves; however, the "divine" Plato would no doubt admonish Publius for failing to provide for the education and training of statesmen. This "sin of omission," incidentally, is viewed by some observers as "the paramount failure of the Founding Fathers." Paul Eidelberg, *The Philosophy of the American Constitution* (New York, 1968), 248. See also Martin Diamond, "Democracy and *The Federalist*: A Reconsideration of the Framers' Intent," *American Political Science Review* 53 (1959), 52–68.

57. Charles R. Kesler, ed., *Saving the Revolution: The Federalist Papers and the American Founding* (New York, 1987), 3.

# THE ESSENTIAL FEDERALIST

# 1

---

# Of First and Last Things

$I$N THEIR COMMENTARIES ON THE *Constitution, the authors of* The Federalist *made a series of persuasive arguments on behalf of that document's basic structure and various provisions. Yet Publius also recognized the need to appeal to his readers in a more direct and urgent manner. Convinced that "nothing less than the existence of the* UNION" *was at stake, Hamilton, Madison, and Jay spared no effort in underscoring the "merits of the Constitution, and the expediency of adopting it." Their remarks in this area were intended to leave the reader with little doubt regarding the one or the other. As a whole, such passages may fairly be described as the "opening statements" and "closing arguments" of Publius' celebrated defense of the Constitution.*

*Most of the selections in this chapter fall under this description. Here it is the concern of Publius to (1) expose the inherent and irreparable defects of the Articles of Confederation; (2) raise the specter of disunion; (3) urge the necessity of furnishing the national government with powers adequate to its task; (4) call for fairness and moderation in debating the merits of the Constitution; (5) appeal to the good sense, patriotism, and shared interests of the American people; (6) admonish those whose opposition to the plan was unprincipled or devoid of substance; (7) defend the intentions and efforts of the Framers; (8) highlight the palpable advantages of adopting the plan; (9) argue against calls for a second convention to "correct" the alleged errors of the first; and (10) declare that a bill*

*of rights was not needed since "the Constitution is itself in every rational sense
. . . A BILL OF RIGHTS."*

*In its treatment of these "first and last things," The Federalist—a work
distinguished by its authors' elevated prose style—soared to the heights of rhetorical eloquence. Against the backdrop of Publius' compelling analysis of the
Constitution, such lofty exhortations served to reinforce his conclusion that "it is
in your interest to adopt it."*

*A number of the following selections do not address the ratification issue
directly, but represent miscellaneous observations which have been included for
their intrinsic value. Some of these are of a general nature and contribute to the
overall "message" of The Federalist. Others speak to more specific concerns
such as slavery, whose significance is largely self-evident.*

AFTER AN UNEQUIVOCAL experience of the inefficacy of the subsisting Federal Government, you are called upon to deliberate on a new Constitution
for the United States of America. The subject speaks its own importance; comprehending in its consequences, nothing less than the existence
of the UNION, the safety and welfare of the parts of which it is composed,
the fate of an empire, in many respects, the most interesting in the world.
It has been frequently remarked, that it seems to have been reserved to
the people of this country, by their conduct and example, to decide the
important question, whether societies of men are really capable or not of
establishing good government from reflection and choice, or whether
they are forever destined to depend for their political constitutions on
accident and force. If there be any truth in the remark, the crisis at which
we are arrived, may with propriety be regarded as the era in which that
decision is to be made; and a wrong election of the part we shall act, may,
in this view, deserve to be considered as the general misfortune of mankind.

This idea will add the inducements of philanthropy to those of patriotism to heighten the solicitude which all considerate and good men
must feel for the event. Happy will it be if our choice should be decided
by a judicious estimate of our true interests, unperplexed and unbiased
by considerations not connected with the public good. But this is a thing
more ardently to be wished than seriously to be expected. The plan offered to our deliberations affects too many particular interests, innovates
upon too many local institutions, not to involve in its discussion a variety
of objects foreign to its merits, and of views, passions and prejudices
little favorable to the discovery of truth. (No. 1)

I AM WELL AWARE that it would be disingenuous to resolve indiscriminately the opposition of any set of men (merely because their situations might subject them to suspicion) into interested or ambitious views. Candor will oblige us to admit, that even such men may be actuated by upright intentions; and it cannot be doubted that much of the opposition [to the Constitution] which has made its appearance, or may hereafter make its appearance, will spring from sources, blameless at least, if not respectable, the honest errors of minds led astray by preconceived jealousies and fears. So numerous indeed and so powerful are the causes which serve to give a false bias to the judgment, that we upon many occasions see wise and good men on the wrong as well as on the right side of questions of the first magnitude to society. This circumstance, if duly attended to, would furnish a lesson of moderation to those who are ever so much persuaded of their being in the right in any controversy. And a further reason for caution, in this respect, might be drawn from the reflection, that we are not always sure that those who advocate the truth are influenced by purer principles than their antagonists. Ambition, avarice, personal animosity, party opposition, and many other motives not more laudable than these, are apt to operate as well upon those who support as upon those who oppose the right side of a question. Were there not even these inducements to moderation, nothing could be more ill-judged than that intolerant spirit, which has at all times characterized political parties. For in politics as in religion, it is equally absurd to aim at making proselytes by fire and sword. Heresies in either can rarely be cured by persecution. (No. 1)

YES, MY COUNTRYMEN, I own to you that, after having given it an attentive consideration, I am clearly of opinion it is your interest to adopt [the Constitution]. I am convinced that this is the safest course for your liberty, your dignity, and your happiness. I effect not reserves which I do not feel. I will not amuse you with an appearance of deliberation when I have decided. I frankly acknowledge to you my convictions, and I will freely lay before you the reasons on which they are founded. The consciousness of good intentions disdains ambiguity. I shall not however multiply professions on this head. My motives must remain in the depository of my own breast. My arguments will be open to all, and may be judged of by all. They shall at least be offered in a spirit which will not disgrace the cause of truth. (No. 1)

NOTHING IS MORE CERTAIN than the indispensable necessity of Government, and it is equally undeniable that whenever and however it is instituted, the people must cede to it some of their natural rights in order to vest it with requisite powers. (No. 2)

IT IS WORTHY OF REMARK that not only the first, but every succeeding Congress, as well as the late Convention, have invariably joined with the people in thinking that the prosperity of America depended on its Union. To preserve and perpetuate it was the great object of the people in forming that Convention, and it is also the great object of the plan which the Convention has advised them to adopt. With what propriety therefore, or for what good purposes, are attempts at this particular period made by some good men to depreciate the importance of the Union? or why is it suggested that three of four confederacies would be better than one? I am persuaded in my own mind, that the people have always thought right on this subject, and that their universal and uniform attachment to the cause of the Union rests on great and weighty reasons . . . (No. 2)

IT HAS OFTEN GIVEN me pleasure to observe that Independent America was not composed of detached and distant territories, but that one connected, fertile, wide spreading country was the portion of our western sons of liberty. Providence has in a particular manner blessed it with a variety of soils and productions, and watered it with innumerable streams for the delight and accommodation of its inhabitants. A succession of navigable waters forms a kind of chain round its borders, as if to bind it together; while the most noble rivers in the world, running at convenient distances, present them with highways for the easy communication of friendly aids, and the mutual transportation and exchange of their various commodities.

With equal pleasure, I have as often taken notice that Providence has been pleased to give this one connected country to one united people, a people descended from the same ancestors, speaking the same language, professing the same religion, attached to the same principles of government, very similar in their manners and customs, and who, by their joint counsels, arms and efforts, fighting side by side throughout a long and bloody war, have nobly established their general Liberty and Independence.

This country and this people seem to have been made for each other, and it appears as if it was the design of Providence, that an inheritance so proper and convenient for a band of brethren, united to each other by the strongest ties, should never be split into a number of unsocial, jealous and alien sovereignties.

Similar sentiments have hitherto prevailed among all orders and denominations of men among us. To all general purposes we have uniformly been one people—each individual citizen everywhere enjoying the same national rights, privileges, and protection. As a nation we have made peace and war—as a nation we have vanquished our common enemies, as a nation we have formed alliances and made treaties, and entered into various compacts and conventions with foreign States.

A strong sense of the value and blessings of Union induced the people, at a very early period, to institute a Federal Government to preserve and perpetuate it. They formed it almost as soon as they had a political existence; nay at a time when their habitations were in flames, when many of their Citizens were bleeding, and when the progress of hostility and desolation left little room for those calm and mature enquiries and reflections, which must ever precede the formation of a wise and well-balanced government for a free people. It is not to be wondered at that a Government instituted in times so inauspicious should on experiment be found greatly deficient and inadequate to the purpose it was intended to answer.

This intelligent people perceived and regretted these defects. Still continuing no less attached to union than enamored of liberty, they observed the danger which immediately threatened the former and more remotely the latter; and being persuaded that ample security for both could only be found in a national Government more wisely framed, they, as with one voice, convened the late Convention at Philadelphia to take that important subject under consideration. (No. 2)

It is not a new observation that the people of any country (if like the Americans, intelligent and well-informed) seldom adopt, and steadily persevere for many years in an erroneous opinion respecting their interests. That consideration naturally tends to create great respect for the high opinion which the people of America have so long and uniformly entertained of the importance of their continuing firmly united under one Federal Government, vested with sufficient powers for all general and national purposes. (No. 3)

The history of Great Britain is the one with which we are in general the best acquainted, and it gives us many useful lessons. We may profit by their experience, without paying the price which it cost them. (No. 5)

A man must be far gone in Utopian speculations who can seriously doubt, that if these States should either be wholly disunited, or only united in partial confederacies, the subdivisions into which they might be thrown would have frequent and violent contests with each other. To presume a want of motives for such contests as an argument against their existence, would be to forget that men are ambitious, vindicative and rapacious. To look for a continuation of harmony between a number of independent, unconnected sovereignties, situated in the same neighborhood, would be to disregard the uniform course of human events, and to set at defiance the accumulated experience of ages. (No. 6)

HAS IT NOT . . . invariably been found, that momentary passions and immediate interests have a more active and imperious control over human conduct than general or remote considerations of policy, utility or justice? Have republics in practice been less addicted to war than monarchies? Are not the former administered by *men* as well as the latter? Are there not aversions, predilections, rivalships, and desires of unjust acquisition that affect nations as well as kings? Are not popular assemblies frequently subject to the impulses of rage, resentment, jealousy, avarice, and of other irregular and violent propensities? Is it not well-known that their determinations are often governed by a few individuals in whom they place confidence, and are of course liable to be tinctured by the passions and views of those individuals? Has commerce hitherto done anything more than change the objects of war? Is not the love of wealth as domineering and enterprising a passion as that of power or glory? Have there not been as many wars founded upon commercial motives, since that has become the prevailing system of nations, as were before occasioned by the cupidity of territory or dominion? Has not the spirit of commerce in many instances administered new incentives to the appetite both for the one and for the other? Let experience, the least fallible guide of human opinions, be appealed to for an answer to these inquiries. (No. 6)

[W]HAT REASON can we have to confide in those reveries which would seduce us into an expectation of peace and cordiality between the members of the present confederacy in a state of separation? Have we not already seen enough of the fallacy and extravagance of those idle theories which have amused us with promises of an exemption from the imperfections, weaknesses and evils incident to society in every shape? Is it not time to awake from the deceitful dream of a golden age, and to adopt as a practical maxim for the direction of our political conduct, that we, as well as the other inhabitants of the globe, are yet remote from the happy empire of perfect wisdom and perfect virtue? (No. 6)

HEARKEN NOT to the unnatural voice which tells you that the people of America, knit together as they are by so many chords of affection, can no longer live together as members of the same family; can no longer continue the mutual guardians of their mutual happiness; can no longer be fellow citizens of one great respectable and flourishing empire. Hearken not to the voice which petulantly tells you that the form of government recommended for your adoption is a novelty in the political world; that it has never yet had a place in the theories of the wildest projectors; that it rashly attempts what it is impossible to accomplish. No my country-men, shut your ears against this unhallowed language. Shut your hearts against the poison which it conveys. The kindred blood which flows in the veins of American citizens, the mingled blood which they have shed in defense of their sacred rights, consecrate their union, and excite hor-ror at the idea of their becoming aliens, rivals, enemies. And if novelties are to be shunned, believe me, the most alarming of all novelties, the most wild of all projects, the most rash of all attempts, is that of rending us in pieces in order to preserve our liberties and promote our happi-ness. But why is the experiment of an extended republic to be rejected merely because it may comprise what is new? Is it not the glory of the people of America that, whilst they have paid a decent regard to the opinions of former times and other nations, they have not suffered a blind veneration for antiquity, for custom, or for names, to overrule the suggestions of their own good sense, the knowledge of their own situa-tion, and the lessons of their own experience? To this manly spirit, posterity will be indebted for the possession, and the world, for the ex-ample of the numerous innovations displayed on the American theater in favor of private rights and public happiness. Had no important step been taken by the leaders of the revolution for which a precedent could not be discovered, no government established of which an exact model did not present itself, the people of the United States might, at this mo-ment, have been numbered among the melancholy victims of misguided councils; must at best have been laboring under the weight of some of those forms which have crushed the liberties of the rest of mankind. Happily for America, happily we trust for the whole human race, they pursued a new and more noble course. They accomplished a revolution which has no parallel in the annals of human society. They reared the fabrics of governments which have no model on the face of the globe. They formed the design of a great confederacy which it is incumbent on their successors to improve and perpetuate. If their works betray imper-fections, we wonder at the fewness of them. If they erred most in the structure of the union, this was the work most difficult to be executed. This is the work which has been new modeled by the act of your Con-vention, and it is that act on which you are now to deliberate and decide. (No. 14)

THE GREAT AND RADICAL vice in the construction of the existing Confederation is in the principle of LEGISLATION for STATES or GOVERNMENTS in their CORPORTATE OR COLLECTIVE CAPACITIES, and as contradistinguished from the INDIVIDUALS of which they consist. (No. 15)

A WEAK CONSTITUTION must necessarily terminate in dissolution for want of proper powers, or the usurpation of powers requisite for the public safety. Whether the usurpation, when once begun, will stop at the salutary point or go forward to the dangerous extreme, must depend on the contingencies of the moment. Tyranny has perhaps oftener grown out of the assumptions of power called for on pressing exigencies by a defective constitution, than by the full exercise of the largest constitutional authorities. (No. 20)

[F]OR NOTHING IS MORE natural to men in office than to look with peculiar deference towards that authority to which they owe their official existence. (No. 22)

NOT TO CONFER in each case a degree of power commensurate to the end would be to violate the most obvious rules of prudence and propriety, and improvidently to trust the great interests of the nation to hands which are disabled from managing them with vigor and success. (No. 23)

FOR THE ABSURDITY must continually stare us in the face, of confiding to a government the direction of the most essential national interests, without daring to trust it with the authorities which are indispensable to their proper and efficient management. Let us not attempt to reconcile contradictions, but firmly embrace a rational alternative. (No. 23)

IF ON THE CONTRARY he happened to be a man of calm and dispassionate feelings—he would indulge a sigh for the frailty of human nature, and would lament that in a matter [i.e., the ratification debate] so interesting to the happiness of millions the true merits of the question should be perplexed and entangled by expedients so unfriendly to an impartial and right determination. Even such a man could hardly forbear remarking that a conduct of this kind has too much the appearance of an intention to mislead the people by alarming their passions rather than to convince them by arguments addressed to their understandings. (No. 24)

FOR IT IS A TRUTH which the experience of all ages has attested, that the people are always most in danger when the means of injuring their rights are in the possession of those of whom they entertain the least suspicion. (No. 25)

[N]ATIONS PAY LITTLE regard to rules and maxims calculated in their very nature to run counter to the necessities of society. Wise politicians will be cautious about fettering the government with restrictions that cannot be observed; because they know that every breach of the fundamental laws, though dictated by necessity, impairs that sacred reverence which ought to be maintained in the breasts of rulers towards the constitution of a country, and forms a precedent for other breaches where the same plea of necessity does not exist at all, or is less urgent and palpable. (No. 25)

IT WAS A THING hardly to be expected, that in a popular revolution the minds of men should stop at that happy mean which marks the salutary boundary between POWER and PRIVILEGE, and combines the energy of government with the security of private rights. (No. 26)

THE CITIZENS OF AMERICA have too much discernment to be argued into anarchy. And I am much mistaken if experience has not wrought a deep and solemn conviction in the public mind, that greater energy of government is essential to the welfare and prosperity of the community. (No. 26)

I BELIEVE IT MAY be laid down as a general rule, that [the people's] confidence in and obedience to a government will commonly be proportioned to the goodness or badness of its administration. (No. 27)

THAT THERE MAY happen cases in which the national government may be necessitated to resort to force cannot be denied. Our own experience has corroborated the lessons taught by the examples of other nations; that emergencies of this sort will sometimes arise in all societies, however constituted; that seditions and insurrections are unhappily maladies as inseparable from the body politic as tumors and eruptions from the natural body; that the idea of governing at all times by the simple force of law (which we have been told is the only admissible principle of republican government) has no place but in the reveries of those political doctors, whose sagacity disdains the admonitions of experimental instruction. (No. 28)

PROJECTS OF USURPATION cannot be masked under pretenses so likely to escape the penetration of select bodies of men as of the people at large. (No. 28)

I BELIEVE IT MAY be regarded as a position warranted by the history of mankind, that *in the usual progress of things, the necessities of a nation in every stage of its existence will be found at least equal to its resources.* (No. 30)

[W]E ARE LIKELY TO experience a common portion of the vicissitudes and calamities which have fallen to the lot of other nations . . . (No. 30)

IN PURSUING THIS enquiry, we must bear in mind that we are not to confine our view to the present period, but to look forward to remote futurity. Constitutions of civil Government are not to be framed upon a calculation of existing exigencies, but upon a combination of these, with the probable exigencies of ages, according to the natural and tried course of human affairs. (No. 34)

THERE OUGHT to be a CAPACITY to provide for future contingencies, as they may happen; and as these are illimitable in their nature, it is impossible safely to limit that capacity. (No. 34)

HAPPY IT IS when the interest which the government has in the preservation of its own power, coincides with a proper distribution of the public burdens, and tends to guard the least wealthy part of the community from oppression! (No. 36)

I FLATTER MYSELF the progress already made [in these papers] will have sufficed to satisfy the candid and judicious part of the community, that some of the objections which have been most strenuously urged against the Constitution, and which were most formidable in their first appearance, are not only destitute of substance, but if they had operated in the formation of the plan, would have rendered it incompetent to the great ends of public happiness and national prosperity. I equally flatter myself that a further and more critical investigation of the system will serve to recommend it still more to every sincere and disinterested advocate for good government, and will leave no doubt with men of this character of the propriety and expediency of adopting it. Happy will it be for ourselves, and most honorable for human nature, if we have wisdom and virtue enough to set so glorious an example to mankind. (No. 36)

[T]HE ULTIMATE OBJECT of these papers is to determine clearly and fully the merits of this Constitution, and the expediency of adopting it . . . (No. 37)

IT IS A MISFORTUNE inseparable from human affairs, that public measures are rarely investigated with that spirit of moderation which is essential to a just estimate of their real tendency to advance or obstruct the public good; and that this spirit is more apt to be diminished than promoted by those occasions which require an unusual exercise of it. (No. 37)

[THESE PAPERS] SOLICIT the attention of those only who add to a sincere zeal for the happiness of their country, a temper favorable to a just estimate of the means of promoting it. (No. 37)

THE REAL WONDER is that so many difficulties should have been surmounted [in framing the Constitution], and surmounted with a unanimity almost as unprecedented as it must have been unexpected. It is impossible for any man of candor to reflect on this circumstance without partaking of the astonishment. It is impossible for the man of pious reflection not to perceive in it a finger of that Almighty hand which has been so frequently and signally extended to our relief in the critical stages of the revolution. (No. 37)

THE HISTORY OF ALMOST all the great councils and consultations held among mankind for reconciling their discordant opinions, assuaging their mutual jealousies, and adjusting their respective interests is a history of factions, contentions, and disappointments, and may be classed among the most dark and degrading pictures which display the infirmities and depravities of the human character. If in a few scattered instances a brighter aspect is presented, they serve only as exceptions to admonish us of the general truth, and by their lustre to darken the gloom of the adverse prospect to which they are contrasted. In revolving the causes from which these exceptions result, and applying them to the particular instance before us, we are necessarily led to two important conclusions. The first is that the Convention must have enjoyed in a very singular degree, an exemption from the pestilential influence of party animosities, the diseases most incident to deliberative bodies and most apt to contaminate their proceedings. The second conclusion is that all the deputations composing the Convention were either satisfactorily accommodated by the final act, or were induced to accede to it by a deep conviction of the necessity of sacrificing private opinions and partial interests to the public good, and by a despair of seeing this necessity diminished by delays or by new experiments. (No. 37)

IT IS A MATTER BOTH of wonder and regret, that those who raise so many objections against the new Constitution should never call to mind the defects of that which is to be exchanged for it. It is not necessary that the former should be perfect; it is sufficient that the latter is more imperfect. No man would refuse to give brass for silver or gold because the latter had some alloy in it; no man would refuse to quit a shattered and tottering habitation for a firm and commodious building, because the latter had not a porch to it; or because some of the rooms might be a little larger or smaller, or the ceiling a little higher or lower than his fancy would have planned them. (No. 38)

IS THE IMPORTATION of slaves permitted by the new Constitution for twenty years? By the old it is permitted for ever. (No. 38)

THE PUBLIC INTEREST, the necessity of the case, imposed upon [the Convention] the task of overleaping their constitutional limits. But is not the fact an alarming proof of the danger resulting from a government which does not possess regular powers commensurate to its objects? A dissolution or usurpation is the dreadful dilemma to which it is continually exposed. (No. 38)

THE STATES WOULD never have appointed a Convention with so much solemnity, nor described its objects with so much latitude, if some *substantial* reform had not been in contemplation. (No. 40)

LET US VIEW THE GROUND on which the Convention stood. It may be collected from their proceedings that they were deeply and unanimously impressed with the crisis which had led their country, almost with one voice, to make so singular and solemn an experiment for correcting the errors of a system by which this crisis had been produced; that they were no less deeply and unanimously convinced that such a reform as they have proposed was absolutely necessary to effect the purposes of their appointment. It could not be unknown to them that the hopes and expectations of the great body of citizens throughout this great empire were turned with the keenest anxiety to the event of their deliberations. They had every reason to believe that the contrary sentiments agitated the minds and bosoms of every external and internal foe to the liberty and prosperity of the United States. (No. 40)

HAD THE CONVENTION . . . instead of exercising a manly confidence in their country by whose confidence they had been so peculiarly distinguished, and of pointing out a system capable in their judgment of securing its happiness, taken the cold and sullen resolution of disappointing its ardent hopes of sacrificing substance to forms, of committing the dearest interests of their country to the uncertainties of delay and the hazard of events, let me ask the man who can raise his mind to one elevated conception, who can awaken in his bosom one patriotic emotion: what judgment ought to have been pronounced by the impartial world, by the friends of mankind, by every virtuous citizen, on the conduct and character of this assembly? Or if there be a man whose propensity to condemn is susceptible of no control, let me then ask: what sentence he has in reserve for the twelve States, who *usurped the power* of sending deputies to the Convention, a body utterly unknown to their constitutions; for Congress, who recommended the appointment of this body, equally unknown to the Confederation?; and for the State of New York in particular, who first urged and then complied with this unauthorized interposition? (No. 40)

[IF THE DELEGATES TO the Convention] exceeded their powers, they were not only warranted but required as the confidential servants of their country by the circumstances in which they were placed to exercise the liberty which they assumed; and that finally, if they had violated both their powers and their obligations in proposing a Constitution, this ought nevertheless to be embraced if it be calculated to accomplish the views and happiness of the people of America. (No. 40)

THE MOMENT OF ITS [the Union's] dissolution will be the date of a new order of things. (No. 41)

[THE] PICTURE OF the consequences of disunion cannot be too highly colored or too often exhibited. Every man who loves peace, every man who loves his country, every man who loves liberty, ought to have it ever before his eyes, that he may cherish in his heart a due attachment to the Union of America, and be able to set a due value on the means of preserving it. (No. 41)

IT WERE DOUBTLESS to be wished that the power of prohibiting the importation of slaves had not been postponed until the year 1808, or rather that it had been suffered to have immediate operation. But it is not difficult to account either for this restriction on the general government, or for the manner in which the whole clause is expressed. It ought to be considered as a great point gained in favor of humanity, that a period of twenty years may terminate forever within these States, a traffic which has so long and so loudly upbraided the barbarism of modern policy . . . Happy would it be for the unfortunate Africans, if an equal prospect lay before them, of being redeemed from the oppressions of their European brethren! (No. 42)

[I]F THE UNION . . . be essential to the security of the people of America against foreign danger; if it be essential to their security against contentions and wars among the different States; if it be essential to guard them against those violent and oppressive factions which embitter the blessings of liberty, and against those military establishments which must gradually poison its very fountain. If, in a word, the Union be essential to the happiness of the people of America, is it not preposterous to urge as an objection to a government without which the objects of the Union cannot be attained, that such a Government may derogate from the importance of the Governments of the individual States? Was then the American revolution effected, was the America confederacy formed, was the precious blood of thousands spilt, and the hard earned substance of millions lavished, not that the people of America should enjoy peace, liberty and safety: but that the Governments of the individual States, that particular municipal establishments, might enjoy a certain extent of power, and be arrayed with certain dignities and attributes of sovereignty? We have heard of the impious doctrine in the Old World that the people were made for kings, not kings for the people. Is the same doctrine to be revived in the new, in another shape; that the solid happiness of the people is to be sacrificed to the views of political institutions of a different form? It is too early for politicians to presume on our forgetting that the public good, the real welfare of the great body of the people, is the supreme object to be pursued; and that no form of Government whatever has any other value than as it may be fitted for the attainment of this object. Were the plan of the Convention adverse to the public happiness, my voice would be, reject the plan. Were the Union itself inconsistent with the public happiness, it would be, abolish the Union. In like manner as far as the sovereignty of the States cannot be reconciled to the happiness of the people, the voice of every good citizen must be, let the former be sacrificed to the latter. (No. 45)

NOTWITHSTANDING THE SUCCESS which has attended the revisions of our established forms of government, and which does so much honor to the virtue and intelligence of the people of America, it must be confessed that the experiments are of too ticklish a nature to be unnecessarily multiplied. We are to recollect that all the existing constitutions were formed in the midst of a danger which repressed the passions most unfriendly to order and concord; of an enthusiastic confidence of the people in their patriotic leaders, which stifled the ordinary diversity of opinions on great national questions; of a universal ardor for new and opposite forms, produced by a universal resentment and indignation against the ancient government; and whilst no spirit of party connected with the changes to be made, or the abuses to be reformed, could mingle its leaven in the operation. The future situations in which we must expect to be usually placed, do not present any equivalent security against the danger which is apprehended. (No. 49)

WE SUBSCRIBE TO THE DOCTRINE . . . that representation relates more immediately to persons, and taxation more immediately to property, and we join in the application of this distinction to the case of our slaves. But we must deny the fact that slaves are considered merely as property, and in no respect whatever as persons. The true state of the case is that they partake of both these qualities; being considered by our laws, in some respects as persons, and in other respects as property. In being compelled to labor not for himself, but for a master; in being vendible by one master to another master; and in being subject at all times to be restrained in his liberty, and chastised in his body by the capricious will of another, the slave may appear to be degraded from the human rank, and classed with those irrational animals which fall under the legal denomination of property. In being protected, on the other hand, in his life and in his limbs against the violence of all others, even the master of his labor and his liberty; and in being punishable himself for all violence committed against others; the slave is no less evidently regarded by the law as a member of the society, not as a part of the irrational creation; as a moral person, not as a mere article of property. The Federal Constitution therefore decides with great propriety on the case of our slaves when it views them in the mixed character of persons and of property. This is in fact their true character. It is the character bestowed on them by the laws under which they live; and it will not be denied that these are the proper criterion, because it is only under the pretext that the laws have transformed the negroes into subjects of property, that a place is disputed them in the computation of numbers. And it is admitted that if the laws were to restore the rights which have been taken away, the negroes could no longer be refused an equal share of representation with the other inhabitants. (No. 54)

THE CONGRESS WHICH conducted us through the Revolution were a less numerous body than their successors will be; they were not chosen by, nor responsible to their fellow citizens at large. Though appointed from year to year, and recallable at pleasure, they were generally continued for three years, and prior to the ratification of the federal articles, for a still longer term. They held their consultations always under the veil of secrecy; they had the sole transaction of our affairs with foreign nations. Through the whole course of the war they had the fate of their country more in their hands, than it is to be hoped will ever be the case with our future representatives. And from the greatness of the prize at stake and the eagerness of the party which lost it, it may well be supposed that the use of other means than force would not have been scrupled. Yet we know by happy experience that the public trust was not betrayed; nor has the purity of our public councils in this particular ever suffered even from the whispers of calumny. (No. 55)

A GOOD GOVERNMENT implies two things; first, fidelity to the object of government, which is the happiness of the people; secondly, a knowledge of the means by which that object can be best attained. Some governments are deficient in both these qualities. Most governments are deficient in the first. I scruple not to assert that in the American governments, too little attention has been paid to the last. The federal Constitution avoids this error; and what merits particular notice, it provides for the last in a mode which increases the security for the first. (No. 62)

IT IS A JUST AND not a new observation, that enemies to particular persons, and opponents to particular measures, seldom confine their censures to such things only in either, as are worthy of blame. Unless on this principle it is difficult to explain the motives of their conduct, who condemn the proposed Constitution in the aggregate, and treat with severity some of the most unexceptionable articles in it. (No. 64)

THERE ARE MEN, who under any circumstances, will have the courage to do their duty at every hazard. (No. 73)

THE ERECTION OF a new government, whatever care or wisdom may distinguish the work, cannot fail to originate questions of intricacy and nicety; and these may in a particular manner be expected to flow from the establishment of a constitution founded upon the total or partial incorporation of a number of distinct sovereignties. 'Tis time only that can mature and perfect so compound a system, can liquidate the meaning of all the parts, and can adjust them to each other in a harmonious and consistent WHOLE. (No. 82)

THE TRUTH IS . . . that the Constitution is itself in every rational sense, and to every useful purpose, A BILL OF RIGHTS. (No. 84)

THE GREAT BULK of the citizens of America, are with reason convinced that union is the basis of their political happiness. Men of sense of all parties now, with few exceptions, agree that it cannot be preserved under the present system, nor without radical alterations; that new and extensive powers ought to be granted to the national head, and that these require a different organization of the federal government, a single body being an unsafe depository of such ample authorities. (No. 84)

THE ADDITIONAL securities to republican government, to liberty and to property, to be derived from the adoption of the plan under consideration, consist chiefly in the restraints which the preservation of the union will impose on local factions and insurrections, and on the ambition of powerful individuals in single states, who might acquire credit and influence enough from leaders and favorites, to become the despots of the people; in the diminution of the opportunities to foreign intrigue, which the dissolution of the confederacy would invite and facilitate; in the prevention of extensive military establishments, which could not fail to grow out of wars between the states in a disunited situation; in the express guarantee of a republican form of government to each; in the absolute and universal exclusion of titles of nobility; and in the precautions against the repetition of those practices on the part of the state governments, which have undermined the foundations of property and credit, have planted mutual distrust in the breasts of all classes of citizens, and have occasioned an almost universal prostration of morals. (No. 85)

LET US NOW PAUSE and ask ourselves whether in the course of these papers, the proposed Constitution has not been satisfactorily vindicated from the aspersions thrown upon it, and whether it has not been shown to be worthy of the public approbation, and necessary to the public safety and prosperity. Every man is bound to answer these questions to himself, according to the best of his conscience and understanding, and to act agreeably to the genuine and sober dictates of his judgment. This is a duty from which nothing can give him a dispensation. 'Tis one that he is called upon, nay, constrained by all the obligations that form the bands of society, to discharge sincerely and honestly. No partial motive, no particular interest, no pride of opinion, no temporary passion or prejudice will justify to himself, to his country, or to his posterity, an improper election of the part he is to act. Let him beware of an obstinate adherence to party. Let him reflect that the object upon which he is to decide is not a particular interest of the community, but the very existence of the nation. (No. 85)

I AM PERSUADED that [the proposed Constitution] is the best which our political situation, habits, and opinions will admit, and superior to any the revolution has produced. (No. 85)

[T]HE SYSTEM, though it may not be perfect in every part, is upon the whole a good one, is the best that the present views and circumstances of the country will permit, and is such a one as promises every species of security which a reasonable people can desire. (No. 85)

I SHOULD ESTEEM it the extreme of imprudence to prolong the precarious state of our national affairs, and to expose the union to the jeopardy of successive experiments, in the chimerical pursuit of a perfect plan. I never expect to see a perfect work from imperfect man. The result of the deliberations of all collective bodies must necessarily be a compound as well of the errors and prejudices, as of the good sense and wisdom of the individuals of whom they are composed. The compacts which are to embrace thirteen distinct states in a common bond of amity and union, must as necessarily be a compromise of as many dissimilar interests and inclinations. How can perfection spring from such materials? (No. 85)

"To BALANCE A large state or society . . . whether monarchial or republican, on general laws, is a work of so great difficulty that no human genius, however comprehensive, is able by the mere dint of reason and reflection, to effect it. The judgments of many must unite in the work: EXPERIENCE must guide their labor: TIME must bring it to perfection: And the FEELING of inconveniences must correct the mistakes which they *inevitably* fall into, in their first trials and experiments."* These judicious reflections contain a lesson of moderation to all the sincere lovers of the union, and ought to put them upon their guard against hazarding anarchy, civil war, a perpetual alienation of the states from each other, and perhaps the military despotism of a victorious demagogue, in the pursuit of what they are not likely to obtain, but from TIME and EXPERIENCE. It may be in me a defect of political fortitude, but I acknowledge that I cannot entertain an equal tranquility with those who affect to treat the dangers of a longer continuance in our present situation as imaginary. A NATION without a NATIONAL GOVERNMENT is, in my view, an awful spectacle. The establishment of a constitution in time of profound peace, by the voluntary consent of a whole people, is a PRODIGY, to the completion of which I look forward with trembling anxiety. (No. 85)

*Hume's Essays, vol. 1, page 28.—The rise of arts and sciences. (Publius)

# 2

# The Science of Politics

WHILE THE AUTHORS OF THE FEDER-
alist *were wary of abstract reasoning in politics, they did believe that the subject
of government was capable of "scientific" treatment. This is particularly evident
in No. 31, where Hamilton places "certain primary [political] truths" on a near
par with the axioms of geometry and mathematics. Such "maxims in ethics and
politics," Hamilton concedes, may not have the same degree of certitude as those
of hard science; but to "a sound and unbiased mind" they are "almost equally
irresistible."*

*The scientific spirit of Publius is also apparent in the general approach or
"method" of* The Federalist—*empirical and largely systematic—and by the
large number of reasoned generalizations it contains on a broad range of political issues. Like everything else in* The Federalist, *these generalizations are
used to "make the case" for the Constitution. Nevertheless, they possess a theoretical (or philosophical) quality which stands in contrast to the predominantly
practical orientation of the papers as a whole. It is largely on the basis of such
passages that one may speak of* The Federalist *as a work of political theory, as
opposed simply to a commentary on the Constitution.*

*As the following selections illustrate, Publius was fully capable of rising
above the politics of the day and addressing perennial questions from a theoretical perspective. In some instances these remarks are informed by a more specific*

*or practical concern. They all, however, contribute to* The Federalist's *"science of politics," a science Publius believed possessed a prescriptive validity.*

IT WILL BE FORGOTTEN, on the one hand, that jealousy is the usual concomitant of violent love, and that the noble enthusiasm of liberty is too apt to be infected with a spirit of narrow and illiberal distrust. On the other hand, it will be equally forgotten that the vigor of government is essential to the security of liberty; that in the contemplation of a sound and well-informed judgment their interest can never be separated; and that a dangerous ambition more often lurks behind the specious mask of zeal for the rights of the people, than under the forbidding appearance of zeal for the firmness and efficiency of government. History will teach us that the former has been found a much more certain road to the introduction of despotism than the latter, and that of those men who have overturned the liberties of republics, the greatest number have begun their career by paying an obsequious court to the people, commencing Demagogues and ending Tyrants. (No. 1)

THE PRIDE OF STATES, as well as of men, naturally disposes them to justify all their actions, and opposes their acknowledging, correcting, or repairing their errors and offenses. (No. 3)

[I]T IS NOT improbable that what has so often happened would, under similar circumstances, happen again. (No. 4)

DISTRUST NATURALLY creates distrust, and by nothing is good will and kind conduct more speedily changed than by invidious jealousies and uncandid imputations, whether expressed or implied. (No. 5)

WHEN THE DIMENSIONS of a State attain to a certain magnitude, it requires the same energy of government and the same forms of administration which are requisite in one of much greater extent. This idea admits not of precise demonstration, because there is no rule by which we can measure the momentum of civil power necessary to the government of any given number of individuals. . . . Civil power properly organized and exerted is capable of diffusing its force to a very great extent, and can in a manner reproduce itself in every part of a great empire by a judicious arrangement of subordinate institutions. (No. 13)

EXPERIENCE IS the oracle of truth, and where its responses are unequivocal, they ought to be conclusive and sacred. (No. 20)

THIS IS ONE of those truths which to a correct and unprejudiced mind carries its own evidence along with it; and it may be obscured, but cannot be made plainer by argument or reasoning. It rests upon axioms as simple as they are universal. The *means* ought to be proportioned to the *end;* the persons from whose agency the attainment of any *end* is expected, ought to possess the *means* by which it is to be attained. (No. 23)

ALL VIOLENT POLICY, contrary to the natural and experienced course of human affairs, defeats itself. (No. 25)

MAN IS VERY MUCH a creature of habit. A thing that rarely strikes his senses will generally have but little influence upon his mind. A government continually at a distance and out of sight can hardly be expected to interest the sensations of the people. (No. 27)

IN DISQUISITIONS OF every kind there are certain primary truths or first principles upon which all subsequent reasonings must depend. These contain an internal evidence which, antecedent to all reflection or combination, command the assent of the mind. Where it produces not this effect, it must proceed either from some defect or disorder in the organs of perception, or from the influence of some strong interest, or passion, or prejudice. Of this nature are the maxims in geometry. . . . Of the same nature are these other maxims in ethics and politics: that there cannot be an effect without a cause; that the means ought to be proportioned to the end; that every power ought to be commensurate with its object; that there ought to be no limitation of a power destined to effect a purpose which is itself incapable of limitation. And there are other truths in the two latter sciences which, if they cannot pretend to rank in the class of axioms, are yet such direct inferences from them, and so obvious in themselves, and so agreeable to the natural and unsophisticated dictates of common sense, that they challenge the assent of a sound and unbiased mind with a degree of force and conviction almost equally irresistible.

The objects of geometrical enquiry are so entirely abstracted from those pursuits which stir up and put in motion the unruly passions of the human heart, that mankind, without difficulty, adopt not only the more simple theorems of the science, but even those abstruse paradoxes which, however they may appear susceptible of demonstration, are at variance with the natural conceptions which the mind, without the aid of philosophy, would be led to entertain upon the subject. The INFINITE DIVISIBILITY of matter, or in other words, the INFINITE divisibility of a FINITE thing, extending even to the minutest atom, is a point agreed among geometricians; though not less incomprehensible to common sense than any of those mysteries in religion, against which the batteries of infidelity have been so industriously levelled.

But in the sciences of morals and politics men are found far less tractable. To a certain degree it is right and useful that this should be the case. Caution and investigation are a necessary armor against error and imposition. But this untractableness may be carried too far, and may degenerate into obstinacy, perverseness, or disingenuity. Though it cannot be pretended that the principles of moral and political knowledge have in general the same degree of certainty with those of the mathematics; yet they have much better claims in this respect than, to judge from the conduct of men in particular situations, we should be disposed to allow them. The obscurity is much oftener in the passions and prejudices of the reasoner than in the subject. Men upon too many occasions do not give their own understandings fair play, but yielding to some untoward bias, they entangle themselves in words and confound themselves in subtleties. (No. 31)

NECESSITY, especially in politics, often occasions false hopes, false reasonings, and a system of measures correspondingly erroneous. (No. 35)

[A] FAULTLESS PLAN was not to be expected. Nor will they barely make allowances for the errors which may be chargeable on the fallibility to which the Convention, as a body of men, were liable; but will keep in mind that they themselves are also but men, and ought not to assume an infallibility in rejudging the fallible opinions of others.

With equal readiness will it be perceived that, besides these inducements to candor, many allowances ought to be made for the difficulties inherent in the very nature of the undertaking referred to the Convention.

The novelty of the undertaking immediately strikes us. It has been shown in the course of these papers that the existing Confederation is founded on principles which are fallacious; that we must consequently change this first foundation, and with it the superstructure resting upon it. It has been shown that the other confederacies, which could be consulted as precedents, have been vitiated by the same erroneous principles, and can therefore furnish no other light than that of beacons which give warning of the course to be shunned, without pointing out that which ought to be pursued. The most that the Convention could do in such a situation was to avoid the errors suggested by the past experience of other countries as well as of our own, and to provide a convenient mode of rectifying their own errors as future experience may unfold them.

Among the difficulties encountered by the Convention, a very important one must have lain in combining the requisite stability and energy in Government with the inviolable attention due to liberty and to the Republican form. Without substantially accomplishing this part of their undertaking, they would have very imperfectly fulfilled the object of their appointment or the expectation of the public. Yet that it could not be easily accomplished will be denied by no one who is unwilling to betray his ignorance of the subject. Energy in Government is essential to that security against external and internal danger, and to that prompt and salutary execution of the laws which enter into the very definition of good Government. Stability in Government is essential to national character and to the advantages annexed to it; as well as to that repose and confidence in the minds of the people, which are among the chief blessings of civil society. An irregular and mutable legislation is not more an evil in itself than it is odious to the people; and it may be pronounced with assurance that the people of this country, enlightened as they are with regard to the nature, and interested, as the great body of them are, in the effects of good Government, will never be satisfied till some remedy be applied to the vicissitudes and uncertainties which characterize the State administrations. On comparing, however, these valuable ingredients with the vital principles of liberty, we must perceive at once the difficulty of mingling them together in their due proportions. The genius of Republican liberty seems to demand, on one side, not only that all power should be derived from the people, but that those entrusted with it should be kept in dependence on the people by a short duration of their appointments; and, that, even during this short period, the trust should be placed not in a few, but in a number of hands. Stability, on the contrary, requires that the hands in which power is lodged should continue for a length of time the same. A frequent change of men will result from a frequent return of elections, and a frequent change of measures from a frequent change of men: whilst energy in Government requires not only a certain duration of power, but the execution of it by a single hand. (No. 37)

NOT LESS ARDUOUS must have been the task of marking the proper line of partition between the authority of the general, and that of the State Governments. Every man will be sensible of this difficulty in proportion as he has been accustomed to contemplate and discriminate objects extensive and complicated in their nature. The faculties of the mind itself have never yet been distinguished and defined with satisfactory precision by all the efforts of the most acute and metaphysical Philosophers. Sense, perception, judgment, desire, volition, memory, imagination are found to be separated by such delicate shapes and minute gradations, that their boundaries have eluded the most subtle investigations, and remain a pregnant source of ingenious disquisition and controversy. The boundaries between the great kingdoms of nature, and still more between the various provinces and lesser portions into which they are subdivided, afford another illustration of the same important truth. The most sagacious and laborious naturalists have never yet succeeded in tracing with certainty the line which separates the district of vegetable life from the neighboring region of unorganized matter, or which marks the termination of the former and the commencement of the animal empire. A still greater obscurity lies in the distinctive characters by which the objects in each of these great departments of nature have been arranged and assorted. When we pass from the works of nature, in which all the delineations are perfectly accurate, and appear to be otherwise only from the imperfection of the eye which surveys them, to the institutions of man, in which the obscurity arises as well from the object itself as from the organ by which it is contemplated, we must perceive the necessity of moderating still farther our expectations and hopes from the efforts of human sagacity. Experience has instructed us that no skill in the science of Government has yet been able to discriminate and define, with sufficient certainty, its three great provinces, the Legislative, Executive and Judiciary; or even the privileges and powers of the different Legislative branches. Questions daily occur in the course of practice which prove the obscurity which reigns in these subjects, and which puzzle the greatest adepts in political science. The experience of ages, with the continued and combined labors of the most enlightened Legislators and jurists, have been equally unsuccessful in delineating the several objects and limits of different codes of laws and different tribunals of justice. (No. 37)

ALL NEW LAWS, though penned with the greatest technical skill, and passed on the fullest and most mature deliberation, are considered as more or less obscure and equivocal until their meaning be liquidated and ascertained by a series of particular discussions and adjudications. Besides the obscurity arising from the complexity of objects, and the imperfection of the human faculties, the medium through which the conceptions of men are conveyed to each other adds a fresh embarrassment. The use of words is to express ideas. Perspicuity, therefore, requires not only that the ideas should be distinctly formed, but that they should be expressed by words distinctly and exclusively appropriated by them. But no language is so copious as to supply words and phrases for every complex idea, or so correct as not to include many equivocally denoting different ideas. Hence, it must happen that however accurately objects may be discriminated in themselves, and however accurately the discrimination may be considered, the definition of them may be rendered inaccurate by the inaccuracy of the terms in which it is delivered. And this unavoidable inaccuracy must be greater or less according to the complexity and novelty of the objects defined. When the Almighty himself condescends to address mankind in their own language, his meaning, luminous as it must be, is rendered dim and doubtful by the cloudy medium through which it is communicated. Here then are three sources of vague and incorrect definitions; indistinctness of the object, imperfection of the organ of conception, inadequateness of the vehicle of ideas. Any one of these must produce a certain degree of obscurity. The Convention, in delineating the boundary between the Federal and State jurisdictions, must have experienced the full effect of them all. (No. 37)

THERE ARE FEATURES in the Constitution which warrant [the supposition] . . . that the Convention must have been compelled to sacrifice theoretical propriety to the force of extraneous considerations. (No. 37)

IF THESE LESSONS teach us, on one hand, to admire the improvement made by America on the ancient mode of preparing and establishing regular plans of government, they serve not less on the other, to admonish us of the hazards and difficulties incident to such experiments, and of the great imprudence of unnecessarily multiplying them.

Is it an unreasonable conjecture that the errors which may be contained in the plan of the Convention are such as have resulted rather from the defect of antecedent experience on this complicated and difficult subject, than from a want of accuracy or care in the investigation of it; and consequently such as will not be ascertained until an actual trial shall have pointed them out? (No. 38)

[T]HE GREAT PRINCIPLES of the Constitution proposed by the Convention may be considered less as absolutely new than as the expansion of principles which are found in the Articles of Confederation. The misfortune under the latter system has been that these principles are so feeble and confined as to justify all the charges of inefficiency which have been urged against it, and to require a degree of enlargement which gives to the new system the aspect of an entire transformation of the old. (No. 40)

[THE CONVENTION] must have reflected, that in all great changes of established governments, forms ought to give way to substance; that a rigid adherence, in such cases, to the former, would render nominal and nugatory the transcendent and precious right of the people to "abolish or alter their governments as to them shall seem most likely to effect their safety and happiness;"* since it is impossible for the people spontane-

*Declaration of Independence (Publius)

ously and universally to move in concert towards their object. And it is therefore essential that such changes be instituted by some *informal and unauthorized propositions*, made by some patriotic and respectable citizen or number of citizens. (No. 40)

THE PRUDENT enquiry, in all cases, ought surely to be not so much *from whom* the advice comes, as whether the advice be *good*. (No. 40)

[C]OOL AND CANDID people will at once reflect that the purest of human blessings must have a portion of alloy in them; that the choice must always be made, if not of the lesser evil, at least of the GREATER, not the PERFECT good; and that in every political institution, a power to advance the public happiness involves a discretion which may be misapplied and abused. They will see, therefore, that in all cases where power is to be conferred, the point first to be decided is whether such a power be necessary to the public good; as the next will be . . . to guard as effectually as possible against a perversion of the power to the public detriment. (No. 41)

A BAD cause seldom fails to betray itself. (No. 41)

[T]HE MILD VOICE of reason, pleading the cause of an enlarged and permanent interest, is but too often drowned before public bodies as well as individuals, by the clamors of an impatient avidity for immediate and immoderate gain. (No. 42)

THAT USEFUL alterations [to the Constitution] will be suggested by experience could not but be foreseen. It was requisite therefore that a mode for introducing them should be provided. The mode preferred by the Convention seems to be stamped with every mark of propriety. It guards equally against that extreme facility which would render the Constitution too mutable, and that extreme difficulty which might perpetuate its discovered faults. It, moreover, equally enables the general and the state governments to originate the amendment or errors as they may be pointed out by the experience on one side or on the other. (No. 43)

IN CASES WHERE it may be doubtful on which side justice lies, what better umpires could be desired by two violent factions, flying to arms and tearing a State to pieces, than the representatives of confederate States not heated by the local flame? To the impartiality of Judges they would unite the affection of friends. Happy would it be if such a remedy for its infirmities, could be enjoyed by all free governments; if a project equally effectual could be established for the universal peace of mankind! (No. 43)

[T]HEORETIC reasoning, in this, as in most other cases, must be qualified by the lessons of practice. (No. 43)

[T]HE GREAT principle of self-preservation, . . . the transcendent law of nature and of nature's God . . . declares that the safety and happiness of society are the objects at which all political institutions aim, and to which all institutions must be sacrificed. (No. 43)

I TAKE NO notice of an unhappy species of population abounding in some of the States, who during the calm of regular government are sunk below the level of men; but who in the tempestuous scenes of civil violence may emerge into the human character, and give a superiority of strength to any party with which they may associate themselves. (No. 43)

BILLS OF ATTAINDER, ex post facto laws, and laws impairing the obligation of contracts are contrary to the first principles of the social compact, and to every principle of sound legislation. (No. 44)

No AXIOM is more clearly established in law or in reason than that wherever the end is required, the means are authorized; wherever a general power to do a thing is given, every particular power necessary for doing it is included. (No. 44)

[T]HE PEOPLE ARE the only legitimate fountain of power, and it is from them that the constitutional charter, under which the several branches of government hold their power, is derived. (No. 49)

IF IT BE TRUE that all governments rest on opinion, it is no less true that the strength of opinion in each individual, and its practical influence on his conduct, depend much on the number which he supposes to have entertained the same opinion. The reason of man, like man himself is timid and cautious when left alone, and acquires firmness and confidence in proportion to the number with which it is associated. When the examples which fortify opinion are *ancient* as well as *numerous*, they are known to have a double effect. In a nation of philosophers, this consideration ought to be disregarded. A reverence for the laws would be sufficiently inculcated by the voice of enlightened reason. But a nation of philosophers is as little to be expected as the philosophical race of kings wished for by Plato. And in every other nation the most rational government will not find it a superfluous advantage to have the prejudices of the community on its side. (No. 49)

[I]T IS THE reason of the public alone that ought to control and regulate the government. The passions ought to be controlled and regulated by the government. (No. 49)

WHEN MEN exercise their reason coolly and freely on a variety of distinct questions, they inevitably fall into different opinions on some of them. When they are governed by a common passion their opinions, if they are so to be called, will be the same. (No. 50)

[A]N EXTINCTION of parties necessarily implies either a universal alarm for the public safety, or an absolute extinction of liberty. (No. 50)

LET US CONSULT experience, the guide that ought always to be followed, whenever it can be found. (No. 52)

No MAN WILL subject himself to the ridicule of pretending that any natural connection subsists between the sun or the seasons, and the period within which human virtue can bear the temptations of power. Happily for mankind, liberty is not in this respect confined to any single point of time, but lies within extremes, which afford sufficient latitude for all the variations which may be required by the various situations and circumstances of civil society. (No. 53)

GOVERNMENT IS instituted no less for the protection of the property than of the persons of individuals. (No. 54)

WHAT CHANGE of circumstances time and a fuller population of our country may produce requires a prophetic spirit to declare, which makes no part of my pretensions. (No. 55)

THE EXPERIENCE of Great Britain . . . presents to mankind so many political lessons, both of the monitory and exemplary kind. (No. 56)

THERE IS A contagion in example which few men have sufficient force of mind to resist. (No. 61)

THE MUTABILITY in the public councils arising from a rapid succession of new members, however qualified they may be, points out in the strongest manner the necessity of some stable institution in the government. Every new election in the states is found to change one half of the representatives. From this change of men must proceed a change of opinions, and from a change of opinions, a change of measures. But a continual change even of good measures is inconsistent with every rule of prudence and every prospect of success. The remark is verified in private life, and becomes more just as well as more important in national transactions. (No. 62)

THE INTERNAL EFFECTS of a mutable policy are still more calamitous. It poisons the blessings of liberty itself. It will be of little avail to the people that the laws are made by men of their own choice, if the laws be so voluminous that they cannot be read, or so incoherent that they cannot be understood; if they be repealed or revised before they are promulgated, or undergo such incessant changes that no man who knows what the law is today can guess what it will be tomorrow. Law is defined to be a rule of action; but how can that be a rule which is little known and less fixed?

Another effect of public instability is the unreasonable advantage it gives to the sagacious, the enterprising and the moneyed few, over the industrious and uninformed mass of the people. Every new regulation concerning commerce or revenue, or in any manner affecting the value of the different species of property, presents a new harvest to those who watch the change, and can trace its consequences; a harvest reared not by themselves but by the toils and cares of the great body of their fellow citizens. This is a state of things in which it may be said with some truth that laws are made for the *few* not for the *many*.

In another point of view, great injury results from an unstable government. The want of confidence in the public councils dampens every useful undertaking, the success and profit of which may depend on a continuance of existing arrangements. What prudent merchant will hazard his fortunes in any new branch of commerce, when he knows not but that his plans may be rendered unlawful before they can be executed? What farmer or manufacturer will lay himself out for the encouragement given to any particular cultivation or establishment, when he can have no assurance that his preparatory labors and advances will not render him a victim to an inconstant government? In a word, no great improvement or laudable enterprise can go forward which requires the auspices of a steady system of national policy.

But the most deplorable effect of all is that diminution of attachment and reverence which steals into the hearts of the people towards a political system which betrays so many marks of infirmity, and disappoints so many of their flattering hopes. No government, any more than an individual, will long be respected without being truly respectable, nor be truly respectable without possessing a certain portion of order and stability. (No. 62)

[N]EW ERRORS as well as new truths often appear. (No. 64)

HOWEVER USEFUL jealousy may be in republics, yet when, like bile in the natural, it abounds too much in the body politic, the eyes of both become very liable to be deceived by the delusive appearances which that malady casts on surrounding objects. (No. 64)

IF MANKIND WERE to resolve to agree in no institution of government until every part of it had been adjusted to the most exact standard of perfection, society would soon become a general scene of anarchy, and the world a desert. Where is the standard of perfection to be found? Who will undertake to unite the discordant opinions of a whole community in the same judgment of it, and to prevail upon one conceited projector to renounce his *infallible* criterion, for the *fallible* criterion of his more *conceited neighbor*? (No. 65)

THOUGH WE CANNOT acquiesce in the political heresy of the poet who says:

> "For forms of government let fools contest;
> that which is best administered is best;"*

yet we may safely pronounce, that the true test of a good government is its aptitude and tendency to produce a good administration. (No. 68)

MEN OFTEN OPPOSE a thing merely because they have had no agency in planning it, or because it may have been planned by those whom they dislike. But if they have been consulted and have happened to disapprove, opposition then becomes in their estimation an indispensable duty of self-love. They seem to think themselves bound in honor and by all the motives of personal infallibility to defeat the success of what has been resolved upon, contrary to their sentiments. Men of upright, benevolent tempers have too many opportunities of remarking with horror, to what desperate lengths this disposition is sometimes carried, and how often the great interests of society are sacrificed to the vanity, to the conceit, and to the obstinacy of individuals who have credit enough to make their passions and their caprices interesting to mankind. (No. 70)

IT IS A GENERAL principle of human nature that a man will be interested in whatever he possesses in proportion to the firmness or precariousness

*This couplet from Alexander Pope's *An Essay on Man* . . . (London, 1758), Epistle III, 30, was frequently quoted in the debate over the ratification of the Constitution. Pope's Epistle was first published in 1733. (Editor)

of the tenure by which he holds it; will be less attached to what he holds by a momentary or uncertain title than to what he enjoys by a durable or certain title; and, of course, will be willing to risk more for the sake of the one than for the sake of the other. This remark is not less applicable to a political privilege, or honor, or trust, than to any article of ordinary property. (No. 71)

IT IS NOT GENERALLY to be expected that men will vary and measures remain uniform. The contrary is the usual course of things. And we need not be apprehensive there will be too much stability while there is even the option of changing; nor need we desire to prohibit the people from continuing their confidence where they think it may be safely placed, and where by constancy on their part they may obviate the fatal inconveniences of fluctuating councils and a variable policy. (No. 72)

AND THE HISTORY of every political establishment in which this principle has prevailed [that a fixed number of legislators, as opposed to a quorum, be required to pass measures] is a history of impotence, perplexity, and disorder. (No. 75)

[I]T WILL RARELY HAPPEN that the advancement of the public service will be the primary object either of party victories or of party negotiations. (No. 76)

THE SUPPOSITION of universal venality in human nature is little less an error in political reasoning than the supposition of universal rectitude. The institution of delegated power implies that there is a portion of virtue and honor among mankind which may be a reasonable foundation of confidence. And experience justifies the theory; it has been found to exist in the most corrupt periods of the most corrupt governments. (No. 76)

THE POSSIBILITY of particular mischiefs can never be viewed by a well-informed mind as a solid objection to a general principle which is calculated to avoid general mischiefs, and to obtain general advantages. (No. 80)

THE TRUTH is that the general GENIUS of a government is all that can be substantially relied upon for permanent effects. Particular provisions, though not altogether useless, have far less virtue and efficacy than are commonly ascribed to them; and the want of them will never be with men of sound discernment a decisive objection to any plan which exhibits the leading characters of a good government. (No. 83)

[LIBERTY OF THE press], whatever fine declarations may be inserted in any constitution respecting it, must altogether depend on public opinion, and on the general spirit of the people and of the government. (No. 84)

FOR MY OWN part, I acknowledge a thorough conviction that any amendments which may, upon mature consideration, be thought useful, will be applicable to the organization of the government, not to the mass of its powers. (No. 85)

# 3

---

# Federalism

T HE DELEGATES TO THE FEDERAL
Convention all agreed that the political system established under the Articles of
Confederation was inadequate to "the exigencies of Government & the preservation of the Union." More specifically, they considered the nation's first
constitution defective because it failed to grant the central authority sufficient
powers to govern effectively. Such views formed the basis of a general consensus
among the delegates regarding the need to strengthen the national government.
This consensus broke down, however, when it came to the actual task of
reconfiguring the Union. At one end of the spectrum were those who wanted to
retain the basic structure of the Articles and simply augment the powers of
Congress in a few select areas. Under this approach, the states would have maintained much of their original status in the Union. At the other end were those
who sought to create a "consolidated" government in which the states would be
reduced to little more than administrative districts of the national authority.
Most of the delegates, however, stood somewhere in the middle. Yet even this
majority was frequently at odds over what Publius would later call the "arduous
. . . task of marking the proper line of partition between the authority of the
general, and that of the State governments."

Much of the difficulty stemmed from the lack of constructive examples
which the Convention might look to for guidance. Indeed, the history of confederated government, ancient and modern, was a dismal record of failure; as Publius

*noted, it was a "beacon . . . which gave a warning of the course to be shunned,*
*without pointing out that which ought to be pursued." This lack of precedent did*
*not, however, prevent the Framers from clearly recognizing the need to modify*
*the basic relationship between the central and state governments. Under the*
*Articles, the states delegated a small number of powers to the national author-*
*ity, but retained in full their "sovereignty, freedom, and independence"—hence*
*"confederation." The Constitution dramatically changed this situation. Not only*
*was the national government significantly empowered at the expense of the states,*
*but the Constitution, federal laws, and treaties were made the "supreme Law of*
*the Land." This meant that in cases of conflict, the lawful measures of the na-*
*tional government would overrule those of the states. It did not, however, entail*
*the obliteration of state sovereignty. As Publius assured his readers, the Consti-*
*tution did not aim at a "consolidated" or unitary government, but "only a partial*
*union or consolidation." Under this arrangement, the states would retain all*
*the "numerous and infinite" powers not delegated to the national authority,*
*whose powers were "few and defined." Within its own sphere of authority, the*
*central government would (unlike under the Articles) act directly on the people.*
*It would also, within this same sphere, have final sovereignty over the states*
*themselves.*

*In contrast to a mere "league of friendship," the Constitution established*
*a federal republic, a "hybrid" form of government partaking of both unitary*
*and confederal elements. What, then, did Publius mean when he observed that*
*the Constitution "is in strictness neither a national nor a federal government,*
*but a composition of both"? If we substitute "unitary" for "national," and*
*"confederal" for "federal" (which were often used interchangeably at this time)*
*his meaning becomes clear. This lack of precision should not be surprising: the*
*Framers had, after all, created (in Madison's words) "a system without prece-*
*dent." Indeed, the "compound republic" embodied in the Constitution stands as*
*America's most unique contribution to the theory and practice of government.*

A DISTINCTION, more subtle than accurate, has been raised between a
*confederacy* and a *consolidation* of the States. The essential characteristic of
the first is said to be the restriction of its authority to the members in
their collective capacities, without reaching to the individuals of whom
they are composed. It is contended that the national council ought to
have no concern with any object of internal administration. An exact
equality of suffrage between the members has also been insisted upon as
a leading feature of a Confederate Government. These positions are in
the main arbitrary; they are supported neither by principle nor precedent. It has indeed happened that governments of this kind have generally

operated in the manner which the distinction, taken notice of, supposes to be inherent in their nature—but there have been in most of them extensive exceptions to the practice which serve to prove, as far as example will go, that there is no absolute rule on the subject. And it will be clearly shown in the course of this investigation, that as far as the principle contended for has prevailed, it has been the cause of incurable disorder and imbecility in the government.

The definition of a *Confederate Republic* seems simply to be, an "assemblage of societies" or an association of two or more States into one State. The extent, modifications, and objects of the Federal authority are mere matters of discretion. So long as the separate organization of the members be not abolished, so long as it exists by a constitutional necessity for local purposes, though it should be in perfect subordination to the general authority of the Union, it would still be, in fact and in theory, an association of States, or a confederacy. The proposed Constitution, so far from implying an abolition of the State Governments, makes them constituent parts of the national sovereignty by allowing them a direct representation in the Senate, and leaves in their possession certain exclusive and very important portions of sovereign power. This fully corresponds, in every rational import of the terms, with the idea of a Federal Government. (No. 9)

[I]T IS TO BE remembered that the general government is not to be charged with the whole power of making and administering laws. Its jurisdiction is limited to certain enumerated objects which concern all the members of the republic, but which are not to be attained by the separate provisions of any. The subordinate governments, which can extend their care to all those other objects which can be separately provided for, will retain their due authority and activity. Were it proposed by the plan of the Convention to abolish the governments of the particular States, its adversaries would have some ground for their objection; though it would not be difficult to show that if they were abolished, the general government would be compelled by the principle of self-preservation, to reinstate them in their proper jurisdiction. (No. 14)

THERE WAS A TIME when we were told that breaches by the States of the regulations of the federal authority were not to be expected—that a sense of common interest would preside over the conduct of the respective members, and would beget a full compliance with all the constitutional requisitions of the Union. This language at the present day would appear as wild as a great part of what we now hear from the same quarter will be thought, when we shall have received further lessons from that best oracle of wisdom, experience. It at all times betrayed an ignorance of the true springs by which human conduct is actuated, and belied the original inducements to the establishment of civil power. Why has government been instituted at all? Because the passions of men will not conform to the dictates of reason and justice without constraint. Has it been found that bodies of men act with more rectitude or greater disinterestedness than individuals? The contrary of this has been inferred by all accurate observers of the conduct of mankind; and the inference is founded upon obvious reasons. Regard to reputation has a less active influence when the infamy of a bad action is to be divided among a number, than when it is to fall singly upon one. A spirit of faction, which is apt to mingle its poison in the deliberations of all bodies of men, will often hurry the persons of whom they are composed into improprieties and excesses for which they would blush in a private capacity.

In addition to all this, there is in the nature of sovereign power an impatience of control that disposes those who are invested with the exercise of it to look with an evil eye upon all external attempts to restrain or direct its operations. From this spirit it happens that in every political association which is formed upon the principle of uniting in a common interest a number of lesser sovereignties, there will be found a kind of eccentric tendency in the subordinate or inferior orbs, by the operation of which there will be a perpetual effort in each to fly off from the common center. This tendency is not difficult to be accounted for. It has its origin in the love of power. Power controlled or abused is almost always the rival and enemy of that power by which it is controlled or abridged. This simple proposition will teach us how little reason there is to expect that the persons entrusted with the administration of the affairs of the particular members of a confederacy, will at all times be ready, with perfect good humor and an unbiased regard to the public weal, to execute the resolutions or decrees of the general authority. The reverse of this results from the constitution of human nature. (No. 15)

THOSE WHO HAVE been conversant in the proceedings of popular assemblies; who have seen how difficult it often is when there is no exterior pressure of circumstances to bring them to harmonious resolutions on important points, will readily conceive how impossible it must be to induce a number of such assemblies, deliberating at a distance from each other, at different times, and under different impressions, long to cooperate in the same views and pursuits. (No. 15)

THE TENDENCY OF the principle of [national] legislation for States, or communities in their political capacities, as it has been exemplified by the experiment we have made of it, is equally attested [to] by the events which have befallen all other governments of the confederate kind, of which we have any account, in exact proportion to its prevalence in those systems. (No. 16)

[I]F IT BE POSSIBLE, at any rate, to construct a Federal Government capable of regulating the common concerns and preserving the general tranquility, it must be founded, as to the objects committed to its care, upon the reverse of the principle contended for by the opponents of the proposed Constitution. It must carry its agency to the persons of the citizens. It must stand in need of no intermediate legislations, but must itself be empowered to employ the arm of the ordinary magistrate to execute its own resolutions. The majesty of the national authority must be manifested through the medium of the Courts of Justice. The government of the Union, like that of each State, must be able to address itself immediately to the hopes and fears of individuals; and to attract to its support, those passions, which have the strongest influence upon the human heart. It must in short, possess all the means, and have a right to resort to all the methods of executing the powers with which it is entrusted, that are possessed and exercised by the governments of the particular States. (No. 16)

[I]F THE EXECUTION of the laws of the national government should not require the intervention of the State Legislatures; if they were to pass into immediate operation upon the citizens themselves, the particular governments could not interrupt their progress without an open and violent exertion of an unconstitutional power. No omissions nor evasions would answer the end. They would be obliged to act, and in such a manner as would leave no doubt that they had encroached on the national rights. An experiment of this nature would always be hazardous—in the face of a constitution in any degree competent to its own defense, and of a people enlightened enough to distinguish between a legal exercise and an illegal usurpation of authority. The success of it would require not merely a factious majority in the Legislature, but the concurrence of the courts of justice, and of the body of the people. If the Judges were not embarked in a conspiracy with the Legislature, they would pronounce the resolutions of such a majority to be contrary to the supreme law of the land, unconstitutional and void. If the people were not tainted with the spirit of their State representatives, they, as the natural guardians of the Constitution, would throw their weight into the national scale and give it a decided preponderancy in the contest. Attempts of this kind would not often be made with levity or rashness because they could sel-

dom be made without danger to the authors; unless in cases of a tyrannical exercise of the Federal authority. (No. 16)

It is a known fact in human nature, that its affections are commonly
weak in proportion to the distance or diffusiveness of the object. Upon
the same principle that a man is more attached to his family than to his
neighborhood, to his neighborhood than to the community at large, the
people of each State would be apt to feel a stronger bias towards their
local governments than towards the government of the Union; unless
the force of that principle should be destroyed by a much better administration of the latter. (No. 17)

It is much to be regretted that such imperfect monuments remain of
this curious political fabric [the Achaean League]. Could its interior structure and regular operation be ascertained, it is probable that more light
would be thrown by it on the science of federal government than by any
of the like experiments with which we are acquainted. (No. 18)

From such a parade of constitutional powers in the representatives and
head of this confederacy [of Germanic states], the natural supposition
would be that it must form an exception to the general character which
belongs to its kindred systems. Nothing would be further from the reality. The fundamental principle, on which it rests, that the [German]
empire is a community of sovereigns; that the Diet is a representation of
sovereigns; and that the laws are addressed to sovereigns; render the
empire a nerveless body; incapable of regulating its own members; insecure against external dangers; and agitated with unceasing fermentations
in its own bowels. (No. 19)

It has not a little contributed to the infirmities of the existing federal
system that it never had a ratification by the People. Resting on no better foundation than the consent of the several Legislatures, it has been
exposed to frequent and intricate questions concerning the validity of its
powers; and has in some instances given birth to the enormous doctrine
of a right of legislative repeal. Owing its ratification to the law of a State,
it has been contended that the same authority may repeal the law by
which it was ratified. However gross a heresy it might be to maintain
that *a party* to *a compact* has a right to revoke that *compact*, the doctrine
itself has had respectable advocates. The possibility of a question of this
nature proves the necessity of laying the foundations of our national government deeper than in the mere sanction of delegated authority. The
fabric of American Empire ought to rest on the solid basis of The Con-

SENT OF THE PEOPLE. The streams of national power ought to flow immediately from that pure original fountain of all legitimate authority. (No. 22)

IT MERITS particular attention . . . that the laws of the confederacy, as to the *enumerated* and *legitimate* objects of its jurisdiction, will become the SUPREME LAW of the land; to the observance of which, all officers legislative, executive and judicial in each State, will be bound by the sanctity of an oath. Thus the Legislatures, Courts, and Magistrates of the respective members will be incorporated into the operations of the national government, *as far as its just and constitutional authority extends*; and will be rendered auxiliary to the enforcement of its laws.* (No. 27)

THE OBSTACLES TO usurpation and the facilities of resistance increase with the increased extent of the state, provided the citizens understand their rights and are disposed to defend them. The natural strength of the people in a large community, in proportion to the artificial strength of the government, is greater than in a small [one]; and of course more competent to a struggle with the attempts of the government to establish a tyranny. But in a confederacy [a federal system] the people, without exaggeration, may be said to be entirely the masters of their own fate. Power being almost always the rival of power, the General Government will at all times stand ready to check the usurpations of the state governments, and these will have the same disposition towards the General Government. The people, by throwing themselves into either scale, will infallibly make it preponderate. If their rights are invaded by either, they can make use of the other as the instrument of redress. How wise will it be in them, by cherishing the Union, to preserve to themselves an advantage which can never be too highly prized! (No. 28)

[WHAT IS BEYOND calculation] must be left to the prudence and firmness of the people, who, as they will hold the scales in their own hands, it is to be hoped, will always take care to preserve the constitutional equilibrium between the General and the State Governments. (No. 31)

BUT AS THE PLAN of the Convention aims only at a partial Union or consolidation, the State Governments would clearly retain all the rights of sovereignty which they before had, and which were not by that act *exclu-*

---

*The sophistry which has been employed to show that this will tend to the destruction of the State Governments will, in its proper place, be fully detected. (Publius) *sively* delegated to the United States. This exclusive delegation, or rather this alienation of State sovereignty, would only exist in three cases: where the Constitution in express terms granted an exclusive authority to the Union; where it granted in one instance an authority to the Union and in another prohibited the States from exercising the like authority; and where it granted an authority to the Union to which a similar authority in the States would be absolutely and totally *contradictory* and *repugnant*. (No. 32)

THE NECESSITY OF a concurrent jurisdiction in certain cases results from the division of the sovereign power (and the rule that all authorities of which the States are not explicitly divested in favor of the Union remain with them in full vigor) is not only a theoretical consequence of that division, but is clearly admitted by the whole tenor of the instrument which contains the articles of the proposed constitution. We there find that notwithstanding the affirmative grants of general authorities, there has been the most pointed care in those cases where it was deemed improper that the like authorities should reside in the States, to insert negative clauses prohibiting the exercise of them by the States. The tenth section of the first article consists altogether of such provisions. (No. 32)

IF THE FEDERAL Government should overpass the just bounds of its authority, and make a tyrannical use of its powers, the people, whose creature it is, must appeal to the standard they have formed, and take such measures to redress the injury done to the Constitution, as the exigency may suggest and prudence justify. (No. 33)

BUT IT IS SAID, that the laws of the Union are to be the *supreme law* of the land. But what inference can be drawn from this, or what would they amount to, if they were not to be supreme? It is evident they would amount to nothing. A LAW, by the very meaning of the term, includes supremacy. It is a rule, which those to whom it is prescribed are bound to observe. This results from every political association. If individuals enter into a state of society, the laws of that society must be the supreme regulator of their conduct. If a number of political societies enter into a larger political society, the laws which the latter may enact, pursuant to the powers entrusted to it by its constitution, must necessarily be supreme over those societies, and the individuals of whom they are composed. It would otherwise be a mere treaty, dependent on the good faith of the parties, and not a government, which is only another word for POLITICAL POWER AND SUPREMACY. But it will not follow from this doctrine that acts of the larger society which are *not pursuant* to its constitutional powers, but which are invasions of the residual authorities of the smaller societies, will become the supreme law of the land. These will be merely acts of usurpation and will deserve to be treated as such. (No. 33)

To ARGUE UPON abstract principles, that this co-ordinate [federal] authority cannot exist, is to set up supposition and theory against fact and reality. However proper such reasonings might be, to show that a thing *ought not to exist*, they are wholly to be rejected, when they are made use of to prove that it does not exist, contrary to the evidence of the fact itself. (No. 34)

[REGARDING ITS authority] the proposed Government cannot be deemed a *national* one, since its jurisdiction extends to certain enumerated objects only, and leaves to the several States a residual and inviolable sovereignty over all other objects. It is true that in controversies relating to the boundary between the two jurisdictions, the tribunal which is ultimately to decide is to be established under the general Government. But this does not change the principle of the case. The decision is to be impartially made according to the rules of the Constitution. . . . Some such tribunal is clearly essential to prevent an appeal to the sword and a dissolution of the compact; and that it ought to be established under the general, rather than under the local Governments. (No. 39)

THE PROPOSED Constitution therefore even when tested by the rules laid down by its antagonists is in strictness neither a national nor a federal constitution, but a composition of both. In its foundation, it is federal, not national; in the sources from which the ordinary powers of the Government are drawn, it is partly federal, and partly national; in the operation of these powers, it is national, not federal; in the extent of them again, it is federal, not national; and finally, in the authoritative mode of introducing amendments, it is neither wholly federal, nor wholly national. (No. 39)

[I]N THE NEW government as in the old, the general powers are limited, and . . . the States in all enumerated cases are left in the enjoyment of their sovereign and independent jurisdiction. (No. 40)

As LONG . . . as the existing republican forms [of government] are continued by the States, they are guaranteed by the Federal Constitution. Whenever the states may choose to substitute other republican forms, they have a right to do so, and to claim the federal guaranty for the latter. The only restriction imposed on them is that they shall not exchange republican for anti-republican constitutions; a restriction which it is presumed will hardly be considered as a grievance. (No. 43)

THE STATE Governments may be regarded as constituent and essential parts of the federal Government, whilst the latter is nowise essential to the operation or organization of the former. (No. 45)

THE POWERS DELEGATED by the proposed Constitution to the Federal Government are few and defined. Those which are to remain in the State Governments are numerous and indefinite. The former will be exercised principally on external objects, as war, peace, negotiation, and foreign commerce, with which last the power of taxation will for the most part be connected. The powers reserved to the several States will extend to all the objects, which in the ordinary course of affairs, concern the lives, liberties, and properties of the people, and the internal order, improvement, and prosperity of the State. (No. 45)

THE FEDERAL AND State Governments are in fact but different agents and trustees of the people, constituted with different powers, and designated for different purposes. (No. 46)

IF WE ARE IN a humor to presume abuses of power, it is as fair to presume them on the part of the State Governments, as on the part of the General Government. And as it is more consonant to the rules of a just theory to entrust the Union with the care of its own existence, than to transfer that care to any other hands, if abuses of power are to be hazarded, on the one side, or on the other, it is more rational to hazard them where the power would naturally be placed, than where in would unnaturally be placed. (No. 59)

[I]T DOES NOT APPEAR to be without some reason that in a compound republic partaking both of the national and federal character, the government ought to be founded on a mixture of the principles of proportional and equal representation. But it is superfluous to try by the standard of theory, a part of the Constitution which is allowed on all hands to be the result not of theory, but "of a spirit of amity, and that mutual deference and concession which the peculiarity of our political situation rendered indispensable."* A common government with powers equal to its objects is called for by the voice, and still more loudly by the political situation of America. A government founded on principles more consonant to the wishes of the larger states is not likely to be obtained from the smaller states. The only option, then, for the former lies be-

---

*Quoted from the letter of the President of the Constitutional Convention (George Washington) to the President of Congress, September 17, 1787. (Editor)

tween the proposed government and a government still more objection-
able. Under this alternative, the advice of prudence must be to embrace
the lesser evil; and instead of indulging a fruitless anticipation of the
possible mischiefs which may ensue, to contemplate rather the advantageous consequences which may qualify the sacrifice.

In this spirit it may be remarked that the equal vote allowed to each
state is at once a constitutional recognition of the portion of sovereignty
remaining in the individual states, and an instrument for preserving that
residual sovereignty. So far the equality ought to be no less acceptable to
the large than to the small states, since they are not less solicitous to
guard by every possible expedient against an improper consolidation of
the states into one simple republic. (No. 62)

WHATEVER PRACTICES may have a tendency to disturb the harmony between the states are proper objects of federal superintendence and control.
(No. 80)

THE POWER OF constituting inferior courts is evidently calculated to obviate the necessity of having recourse to the Supreme Court in every case
of federal cognizance. It is intended to enable the national government
to institute or *authorize* in each state or district of the United States, a
tribunal competent to the determination of matters of national jurisdiction within its limits. (No. 81)

[T]HE STATES WILL retain all *preexisting* authorities which may not be
exclusively delegated to the federal head; and . . . this exclusive delegation can only exist in one of three cases: where an exclusive authority is
in express terms granted to the union; or where a particular authority is
granted to the union, and the exercise of a like authority is prohibited to
the states; or where an authority is granted to the union with which a
similar authority in the states would be utterly incompatible. Though
these principles may not apply with the same force to the judiciary as to
the legislative power, yet I am inclined to think that they are in the main
just with respect to the former as well as the latter. And under this impression, I shall lay it down as a rule, that the state courts will *retain* the
jurisdiction they now have, unless it appears to be taken away in one of
the enumerated modes. (No. 82)

# 4

---

# Separation of Powers
# and
# Checks and Balances

WHEN PUBLIUS OBSERVED THAT *"[t]he accumulation of all powers legislative, executive, and judicial in the same hands . . . may be justly pronounced the very definition of tyranny," he spoke for nearly all Americans. Conversely, the idea that "power should be separate and distinct" and subject to "balances and checks" was a "political truth" no less "self-evident" than the right to "life, liberty, and the pursuit of happiness"—so self-evident that the Framers felt no need to refer explicitly to "separation of powers" or "checks and balances" in the new Constitution. The former is implicit in the very structure of that document, whose first three Articles outline the respective powers of the legislative, executive, and judicial branches of the federal government. The latter is clearly apparent in such provisions as the executive veto, the "advice and consent" role of the Senate, and the House of Representatives' power of impeachment.*

*For the Framers, it was not sufficient merely to limit the power of government; it was also necessary to divide that power and place internal checks upon its exercise. Since "power is of an encroaching nature," Publius notes, it needs be separated into its "several classes," which in turn must possess "some practical security . . . against the invasion of the others." In doing just this, the Framers created a government whose basic structure and internal design made the concentration of all powers a virtual impossibility.*

*As Publius observes, the Constitution does not create a rigid separation of powers. Such an arrangement would not only have destroyed the necessary unity of government, but would have rendered each branch defenseless against the encroachments of the others. For this reason the Framers incorporated a number of "checks and balances" into the Constitution. It is therefore more accurate to speak of a system of* connected *or* blended *powers in reference to the structure and workings of the three branches of government. "Unless these departments be so far connected and blended, as to give to each a constitutional control over the others," Publius writes, "the degree of separation which the maxim requires, as essential to free government, can never in practice be duly maintained."*

*In the selections which follow, the reader will note that Publius was particularly concerned with checking the legislative power of the federal government. This concern was prompted by the undue predominance of many of the state legislatures during and after the Revolutionary War. In contrast to the doctrine of legislative supremacy, which prevailed in the early years of the Republic, the Framers created three "co-equal" branches of government and equipped each with the means of defending itself against incursions by the others. This did not mean that the three branches were "equal" in all respects; indeed, it was widely assumed that Congress would play a leading role in national affairs. Yet the Framers placed substantial limits on Congress, and elevated the federal executive and judiciary to the status of "co-ordinate" branches of government. In doing so, they provided a remedy for the imbalance which had plagued many of the first state constitutions and supplied a model for those which followed.*

*The following selections include the famous* Federalist No. 51, *which has been reproduced in its entirety. Here Madison provides a classic analysis of separation of powers and checks and balances, and contributes some of the most memorable passages in all political literature.*

No POLITICAL TRUTH is certainly of greater intrinsic value or is stamped with the authority of more enlightened patrons of liberty than [the separation of powers]. The accumulation of all powers legislative, executive, and judicial in the same hands—whether of one, a few, or many and whether hereditary, self-appointed, or elective—may justly be pronounced the very definition of tyranny. (No. 47)

THE ORACLE WHO is always consulted and cited on this subject [separation of powers] is the celebrated Montesquieu. If he be not the author of this invaluable precept in the science of politics, he has the merit at least of displaying and recommending it most effectually to the attention of mankind. (No. 47)

[U]NLESS THESE departments [three branches of government] be so far connected and blended as to give to each a constitutional control over the others, the degree of separation which the maxim requires as essential to a free government can never in practice be duly maintained. (No. 48)

IT IS AGREED on all sides that the powers properly belonging to one of the departments ought not to be directly or completely administered by either of the other departments. It is equally evident that neither of them ought to possess, directly or indirectly, an overruling influence over the others in the administration of their respective powers. It will not be denied that power is of an encroaching nature, and that it ought to be effectually restrained from passing the limits assigned to it. After discriminating, therefore, in theory the several classes of power—as they may in their nature be legislative, executive, or judicial—the next and most difficult task is to provide some practical security for each against the invasion of the others. (No. 48)

[A] MERE demarcation on parchment of the constitutional limits of the several department is not a sufficient guard against those encroachments which lead to a tyrannical concentration of all the powers of government in the same hands. (No. 48)

To WHAT expedient, then, shall we finally resort for maintaining in practice the necessary partition of power among the several departments as laid down in the Constitution? The only answer that can be given is that, as all these exterior provisions are found to be inadequate, the defect must be supplied by so contriving the interior structure of the government, as that its several constituent parts may, by their mutual relations, be the means of keeping each other in their proper places. Without presuming to undertake a full development of this important idea, I will hazard a few general observations which may perhaps place it in a clearer light, and enable us to form a more correct judgment of the principles and structure of the government planned by the Convention.

In order to lay a due foundation for that separate and distinct exercise of the different powers of government, which to a certain extent is admitted on all hands to be essential to the preservation of liberty, it is evident that each department should have a will of its own; and consequently should be so constituted that the members of each should have as little agency as possible in the appointment of the members of the others. Were this principle rigorously adhered to, it would require that all the appointments for the supreme executive, legislative, and judicial magistracies should be drawn from the same fountain of authority, the people, through channels, having no communication whatever with one another. Perhaps such a plan of constructing the several departments would be less difficult in practice than it may in contemplation appear. Some difficulties, however, and some additional expense would attend the execution of it. Some deviations, therefore, from the principle must be admitted. In the constitution of the judicial department in particular, it might be inexpedient to insist rigorously on the principle; first, because peculiar qualifications being essential in the members, the primary consideration ought to be to select that mode of choice which best secures these qualifications; secondly, because the permanent tenure by which the appointments are held in that department must soon destroy all sense of dependence on the authority conferring them.

It is equally evident that the members of each department should be as little dependent as possible on those of the others for the emoluments annexed to their offices. Were the executive magistrate or the judges not independent of the legislature in this particular, their independence in every other would be merely nominal.

But the great security against a gradual concentration of the several powers in the same department consists in giving to those who administer each department the necessary constitutional means, and personal motives, to resist encroachments of the others. The provision for defense must in this, as in all other cases, be made commensurate to the danger of attack. Ambition must be made to counteract ambition. The interest of the man must be connected with the constitutional rights of the place. It may be a reflection on human nature, that such devices should be necessary to control the abuses of government. But what is government itself but the greatest of all reflections on human nature? If men were angels, no government would be necessary. If angels were to govern men, neither external nor internal controls on government would be necessary. In framing a government which is to be administered by men over men, the great difficulty lies in this: You must first enable the government to control the governed, and in the next place, oblige it to control itself. A dependence on the people is, no doubt, the primary control on the government; but experience has taught mankind the necessity of auxiliary precautions.

This policy of supplying by opposite and rival interests, the defect of better motives, might be traced through the whole system of human affairs, private as well as public. We see it particularly displayed in all the subordinate distributions of power, where the constant aim is to divide and arrange the several offices in such a manner as that each may be a check on the other; that the private interest of every individual may be a sentinel over the public rights. These inventions of prudence cannot be less requisite in the distribution of the supreme powers of the state.

But it is not possible to give to each department an equal power of self-defense. In republican government the legislative authority necessarily predominates. The remedy for this inconvenience is to divide the legislature into different branches; and to render them by different modes of election, and different principles of action, as little connected with each other as the nature of their common functions, and their common dependence on the society will admit. It may even be necessary to guard against dangerous encroachments by still further precautions. As the weight of the legislative authority requires that it should be thus divided, the weakness of the executive may require, on the other hand, that it should be fortified. An absolute negative [veto] on the legislature appears at first view to be the natural defense with which the executive magistrate should be armed. But perhaps it would be neither altogether safe, nor alone sufficient. On ordinary occasions, it might not be exerted with the requisite firmness; and on extraordinary occasions, it might be perfidiously abused. May not this defect of an absolute negative be supplied by some qualified connection between the weaker department, and the weaker branch of the stronger department, by which the latter may be led to support the constitutional rights of the former, without being too much detached from the rights of its own department?

If the principles of which these observations are founded be just, as I persuade myself they are, and they be applied as a criterion to the several state constitutions, and to the federal constitution, it will be found that if the latter does not perfectly correspond with them, the former are infinitely less able to bear such a test.

There are, moreover, two considerations particularly applicable to the federal system of America, which place that system in a very interesting point of view.

*First*. In a single republic all the power surrendered by the people is submitted to the administration of a single government, and usurpations are guarded against by a division of the government into distinct and separate departments. In the compound republic of America, the power surrendered by the people is first divided between two distinct governments, and then the portion allotted to each [is] subdivided among distinct and separate departments. Hence a double security arises to the rights of the people. The different governments will control each other at the same time that each will be controlled by itself.

*Second*. It is of great importance in a republic not only to guard the society against the oppression of its rulers, but to guard one part of the society against the injustice of the other part. Different interests necessarily exist in different classes of citizens. If a majority be united by a common interest, the rights of the minority will be insecure. There are but two methods of providing against this evil: The one by creating a will in the community independent of the majority, that is, of the society itself; the other by comprehending in the society so many separate descriptions of citizens as will render an unjust combination of a majority of the whole very improbable, if not impracticable. The first method prevails in all governments possessing an hereditary or self-appointed authority. This at best is but a precarious security; because a power independent of the society may as well espouse the unjust views of the major, as the rightful interests of the minor party, and may possibly be turned against both parties. The second method will be exemplified in the federal republic of the United States. Whilst all authority in it will be derived from and dependent on the society, the society itself will be broken into so many parts, interests and classes of citizens, that the rights of individuals or of the minority, will be in little danger from interested combinations of the majority. In a free government, the security for civil rights must be the same as that for religious rights. It consists in the one case in the multiplicity of interests, and in the other, in the multiplicity of sects. The degree of security in both cases will depend on the number of interests and sects; and this may be presumed to depend on the extent of country and number of people comprehended under the same government. This view of the subject must particularly recommend a proper federal system to all the sincere and considerate friends of republican government. Since it shows that in exact proportion as the territory of the union may be formed into more circumscribed confederacies or states, oppressive combinations of a majority will be facilitated. The best security under the republican form for the rights of every class of citizens, will be diminished, and consequently the stability and independence of some member of the government, the only other security, must be proportionally increased. Justice is the end of government. It is the end of civil society. It ever has been, and ever will be pursued until it be obtained, or until liberty be lost in the pursuit. In a society under the forms of which the stronger faction can readily unite and oppress the weaker, anarchy may as truly be said to reign as in a state of nature, where the weaker individual is not secured against the violence of the stronger. And as in the latter state even the stronger individuals are prompted by the uncertainty of their condition to submit to a government which may protect the weak as well as themselves. So in the former state will the more powerful factions or parties be gradually induced by a like motive to wish for a government which will protect all parties, the weaker as well as the more powerful. It can be little doubted that if the state of Rhode Island was separated from the confederacy and left to itself, the insecurity of rights under the popular form of government within such narrow limits would be displayed by such reiterated oppressions of factious majorities, that some power altogether independent of the people would soon be called for by the voice of the very factions whose misrule had proved the necessity of it. In the extended republic of the United States, and among the great variety of interests, parties, and sects which it embraces, a coalition of a majority of the whole society could seldom take place on any other principles than those of justice and the general good; and there being thus less danger to a minor from the will of the major party, there must be less pretext also to provide for the security of the former, by introducing into the government a will not dependent on the latter; or in other words, a will independent of society itself. It is no less certain than it is important, notwithstanding the contrary opinions which have been entertained, that the larger the society, provided it lie within a practicable sphere, the more duly capable it will be of self-government. And happily for the *republican cause*, the practicable sphere may be carried to a very great extent by a judicious modification and mixture of the *federal principle*. (No. 51)

ALL CONSTITUTIONAL acts of power, whether in the executive or in the judicial departments, have as much legal validity and obligation as if they proceeded from the legislature; and, therefore, whatever name be given to the power of making treaties, or however obligatory they may be when made, certain it is that the people may with much propriety commit the power to a distinct body from the legislature, the executive, or the judicial. (No. 64)

[THE] PARTIAL intermixture [of the three branches of government] is even in some cases not only proper, but necessary to the mutual defense of the several members of the government against each other. An absolute or qualified negative in the executive upon the acts of the legislative body is admitted by the ablest adepts in political science to be an indispensable barrier against the encroachments of the latter upon the former. (No. 66)

THE SAME RULE which teaches the propriety of a partition between the various branches of power, teaches us likewise that this partition ought to be so contrived as to render the one independent of the other. To what purpose separate the executive or the judiciary from the legislative, if both the executive and the judiciary are so constituted as to be at the absolute devotion of the legislative? Such a separation must be merely

nominal and incapable of producing the ends for which it was established. It is one thing to be subordinate to the laws, and another to be
dependent on the legislative body. The first comports with, the last vio-
lates, the fundamental principles of good government, and whatever may
be the forms of the constitution, unites all power in the same hands. The
tendency of the legislative authority to absorb every other has been fully
displayed and illustrated by examples. . . . In governments purely republican, this tendency is almost irresistible. The representatives of the people
in a popular assembly seem sometimes to fancy that they are the people
themselves, and betray strong symptoms of impatience and disgust at
the least sign of opposition from any other quarter; as if the exercise of
its rights by either the executive or judiciary were a breach of their privilege and an outrage to their dignity. They often appear disposed to exert
an imperious control over the other departments; and as they commonly
have the people on their side, they always act with such momentum as to
make it very difficult for the other members of the government to maintain a balance of the constitution. (No. 71)

THE PROPENSITY of the legislative department to intrude upon the rights,
and to absorb the powers of the other departments, has been already
suggested and repeated; the insufficiency of a mere parchment delinea-
tion of the boundaries of each has also been remarked upon; and the
necessity of furnishing each with constitutional arms for its own defense
has been inferred and proved. From these clear and indubitable principles results the propriety of a negative, either absolute or qualified, in
the executive upon the acts of the legislative branches. Without the one
or the other, the former would be absolutely unable to defend himself
against the depredations of the latter. He might gradually be stripped of
his authorities by successive resolutions, or annihilated by a single vote.
And in the one mode or the other, the legislative and executive powers
might speedily come to be blended in the same hands. If even no propensity had ever discovered itself in the legislative body to invade the
rights of the executive, the rules of just reasoning and theoretic propriety would of themselves teach us that the one ought not to be left at the
mercy of the other, but ought to possess a constitutional and effectual
power of self-defense.

   But the power in question has a further use. It not only serves as a
shield to the executive, but it furnishes an additional security against the
enaction of improper laws. It establishes a salutary check upon the legislative body calculated to guard the community against the effects of
faction, precipitancy, or of any impulse unfriendly to the public good
which may happen to influence a majority of that body.

The propriety of a negative has upon some occasions been combated by an observation that it was not to be presumed a single man would possess more virtue or wisdom than a number of men; and that unless this presumption should be entertained, it would be improper to give the executive magistrate any species of control over the legislative body.

But this observation, when examined, will appear rather specious than solid. The propriety of the thing does not turn upon the supposition of superior wisdom or virtue in the executive, but upon the supposition that the legislative will not be infallible; that the love of power may sometimes betray it into a disposition to encroach upon the rights of the other members of the government; that a spirit of faction may sometimes pervert its deliberations; that impressions of the moment may sometimes hurry it into measures which itself, on maturer reflection, would condemn. The primary inducement to conferring the power in question upon the executive is to enable him to defend himself; the secondary one is to increase the chances in favor of the community against the passing of bad laws through haste, inadvertence, or design. The oftener a measure is brought under examination, the greater the diversity in the situations of those who are to examine it, the less must be the danger of those errors which flow from want of due deliberation, or of those missteps which proceed from the contagion of some common passion or interest. It is far less probable that culpable views of any kind should infect all the parts of the government at the same moment, and in relation to the same object, than that they should by turns govern and mislead every one of them.

It may perhaps be said that the power of preventing bad laws includes that of preventing good ones; and may be used to the one purpose as well as to the other. But this objection will have little weight with those who can properly estimate the mischiefs of that inconstancy and mutability in the laws which form the greatest blemish in the character and genius of our governments. They will consider every institution calculated to restrain the excess of law-making, and to keep things in the same state in which they may happen to be at any given period, as much more likely to do good than harm, because it is favorable to greater stability in the system of legislation. The injury which may possibly be done by defeating a few good laws will be amply compensated by the advantage of preventing a number of bad ones. (No. 73)

IT IS TO be hoped that it will not often happen that improper views will govern so large a proportion as two-thirds of both branches of the Legislature at the same time; and this too in defiance of the counterpoising weight of the executive. It is at any rate far less probable that this should be the case, than that such views should taint the resolutions and conduct of a bare majority. A power of this nature in the executive will often have a silent and unperceived though forcible operation. When men engaged in unjustifiable pursuits are aware that obstructions may come from a quarter which they cannot control, they will often be restrained, by the bare apprehension of opposition, from doing what they would with eagerness rush into if no such external impediments were to be feared. (No. 73)

THE ESSENCE of the legislative authority is to enact laws, or in other words, to prescribe rules for the regulation of the society. While the execution of the laws and the employment of the common strength, either for this purpose or for the common defense, seem to comprise all the functions of the executive magistrate. The power of making treaties is plainly neither the one nor the other. It relates neither to the execution of the subsisting laws, nor to the enaction of new ones, and still less to an exertion of the common strength. Its objects are CONTRACTS with foreign nations which have the force of law, but derive it from the obligations of good faith. They are not rules prescribed by the sovereign to the subject, but agreements between sovereign and sovereign. The power in question seems, therefore, to form a distinct department, and to belong properly neither to the legislative nor to the executive. The qualities elsewhere detailed as indispensable in the management of foreign negotiations, point out the executive as the most fit agent in those transactions; while the vast importance of the trust, and the operation of treaties as laws, plead strongly for the participation of the whole or a part of the legislative body in the office of making them. (No. 75)

IT MUST indeed be clear to a demonstration, that the joint possession of the power in question [treaty-making] by the president and senate would afford a greater prospect of security than the separate possession of it by either of them. (No. 75)

THOUGH IT might . . . be allowable to suppose that the Executive might occasionally influence some individuals in the Senate; yet the supposition that he could in general purchase the integrity of the whole body would be forced and improbable. A man disposed to view human nature as it is, without either flattering its virtues or exaggerating its vices, will see sufficient ground of confidence in the probity of the Senate to rest satisfied not only that it will be impracticable to the Executive to corrupt or seduce a majority of its members, but that the necessity of its cooperation in the business of appointments will be a considerable and salutary restraint upon the conduct of that magistrate. (No. 76)

[T]HE POWER which can *originate* the disposition of honors and emoluments [the president] is more likely to attract than to be attracted by the POWER which can merely obstruct their course [the senate]. If by influencing the president be meant *restraining* him, this is precisely what must have been intended [by the Convention]. And it has been shown that the restraint would be salutary, at the same time that it would not be such as to destroy a single advantage to be looked for from the uncontrolled agency of that magistrate. The right of nomination would produce all the good, without the ill. (No. 77)

A BODY so fluctuating, and at the same time so numerous [as the House of Representatives] can never be deemed proper [in sharing with the Senate] the exercise of that power [of confirming presidential appointments]. Its unfitness will appear manifest to all, when it is recollected that in half a century it may consist of three or four hundred persons. All the advantages of the stability, both of the executive and of the Senate, would be defeated by this union, and infinite delays and embarrassments would be occasioned. (No. 77)

NEXT TO permanency in office, nothing can contribute more to the independence of the judges than a fixed provision for their support. The remark made in relation to the president is equally applicable here. In the general course of human nature, *a power over a man's subsistence amounts to a power over his will.* And we can never hope to see realized in practice the complete separation of the judicial from the legislative power in any system which leaves the former dependent for pecuniary resources on the occasional grants of the latter. The enlightened friends to good government in every state, have seen cause to lament the want of precise and explicit precautions in the state constitutions on this head. (No. 79)

[T]HE CONSTITUTION ought to be the standard of construction for the laws, and that wherever there is an evident opposition, the laws ought to give place to the Constitution. But this doctrine is not deducible from any circumstance peculiar to the plan of the Convention, but from the general theory of a limited constitution. (No. 81)

A LEGISLATURE, without exceeding its province, cannot reverse a [judicial] determination once made in a particular case, though it may prescribe a new rule for future cases. This is the principle, and it applies in all its consequences, exactly in the same manner and extent to the state governments as to the national government. (No. 81)

[T]HE SUPPOSED danger of judicial encroachments on the legislative authority, which has been upon many occasions reiterated, is in reality a phantom. Particular misconstructions and contraventions of the will of the legislature may now and then happen; but they can never be so extensive as to amount to an inconvenience, or in any sensible degree to affect the order of the political system. This may be inferred with certainty from the general nature of the judicial power; from the objects to which it relates; from the manner in which it is exercised; from its comparative weakness, and from its total incapacity to support its usurpations by force. And the inference is greatly fortified by the consideration of the important constitutional check, which the power of instituting impeachments in one part of the legislative body, and of determining upon them in the other, would give to that body upon the members of the judicial department. This is alone a complete security. There never can be danger that the judges, by a series of deliberate usurpations on the authority of the legislature, would hazard the united resentment of the body entrusted with it while this body was possessed of the means of punishing their presumption by degrading them from their stations. While this ought to remove all apprehensions on the subject, it affords at the same time a cogent argument for constituting the Senate a court for the trial of impeachments. (No. 81)

# 5

# Republicanism, Representation, and the Legislature

Antifederalists frequently *charged that the Constitution would create a government incompatible with the existence of the states and hostile to the liberties of the people. Publius addressed both concerns by emphasizing the limited nature of the general government and the federal dimension of the proposed union. His remarks on republicanism and representation were much to the same purpose. Here Publius assured his readers that the Constitution created neither a monarchy, an aristocracy, nor even a democracy, but rather a* republic, *which he defined as "a government which derives all its powers directly or indirectly from the great body of the people, and is administered by persons holding offices during pleasure, for a limited period of time, or during good behavior." The Constitution was therefore best described as embodying a "representative republic."*

*Publius also confronted the Antifederalist assertion that the national government would favor the privileged few at the expense of ordinary citizens, and that members of the Congress would be under no compulsion to remain faithful to their constituents. In response, he noted that Congress would invariably contain a cross-section of representatives who would speak on behalf of the broader interests of society. More fundamentally, legislators who served for a limited term and were dependent on the people for re-election would have little incentive to act contrary to the interests of their constituents. "Duty, gratitude, interest,*

*[and] ambition itself" would ensure the fidelity of the nation's elected represen-*
*tatives.*

*In addition to these constraints, Publius also pointed to the institutional*
*checks of frequent and regular elections, the necessary concurrence of both House*
*and Senate in making laws, and the Constitution itself, which tacitly forbade*
*the enactment of any measure contrary to the fundamental law. Moreover, the*
*Constitution contained "[n]o qualification of wealth, birth, or religious faith, or*
*. . . civil profession" for holding national office. Such provisions, Publius in-*
*sisted, constituted "the genuine and the characteristic means by which Republican*
*Government provides for the liberty and happiness of the people."*

*In a more positive vein, Publius asserted that an "extended republic" such*
*as the United States was the "proper cure" for the dangers to individual liberty*
*long associated with popular government. Contrary to the prevalent view that a*
*republic could only exist in a small geographic area with a homogenous popula-*
*tion, Madison argued that an extensive territory under the governance of*
*republican institutions was ideally suited to countering the gravest threat to*
*individual rights and liberties: the tyranny of an "interested and overbearing*
*majority." While the formation of hostile "interests" or "factions" was inevi-*
*table in a free society, Madison believed that the federal system embodied in the*
*Constitution would render such combinations benign. This aspect of the pro-*
*posed union, "its tendency to break and control the violence of factions," was*
*perhaps the most important feature recommending the Constitution, for it prom-*
*ised "a Republican remedy for the diseases most incident to Republican*
*Government."*

*Madison's discussion of faction and the extended republic appears in* Federalist *No. 10, which has become the most famous of the papers. On the basis of*
*No. 10, Madison is often credited with originating the theory of pluralism and*
*interest-group politics. It has been reproduced here in full.*

A FIRM UNION will be of the utmost moment to the peace and liberty of
the States as a barrier against domestic faction and insurrection. It is
impossible to read the history of the petty republics of Greece and Italy,
without feeling sensations of horror and disgust at the distractions with
which they were continually agitated, and at the rapid succession of revolutions by which they were kept in a state of perpetual vibration between
the extremes of tyranny and anarchy. If they exhibit occasional calms,
these only serve as short-lived contrasts to the furious storms that are to
succeed. If now and then intervals of felicity open themselves to view, we
behold them with a mixture of regret arising from the reflection that the
pleasing scenes before us are soon to be overwhelmed by the tempestu-

ous waves of sedition and party rage. If momentary rays of glory break forth from the gloom, while they dazzle us with a transient and fleeting brilliancy, they at the same time admonish us to lament that the vices of government should pervert the direction and tarnish the luster of those bright talents and exalted endowments, for which the favored soils that produced them have been so justly celebrated. (No. 9)

THE SCIENCE of politics . . . like most other sciences, has received great improvement. The efficacy of various principles is now well understood, which were either not known at all, or imperfectly known to the ancients. The regular distribution of power into distinct departments; the introduction of legislative balances and checks; the institution of courts composed of judges, holding their offices during good behavior; the representation of the people in the legislature by deputies of their own election: these are either wholly new discoveries or have made their principal progress towards perfection in modern times. They are means, and powerful means, by which the excellencies of republican government may be retained and its imperfections lessened or avoided. To this catalogue of circumstances that tend to the amelioration of popular systems of civil government, I shall venture, however novel it may appear to some, to add one more on a principle which has been made the foundation of an objection to the new Constitution: I mean the ENLARGEMENT of the ORBIT within which such systems are to revolve either in respect to the dimensions of a single State, or to the consolidation of several smaller States into one great confederacy. (No. 9)

THE UTILITY OF a confederacy, as well to suppress faction and to guard the internal tranquility of States as to increase their external force and security, is in reality not a new idea. It has been practiced upon in different countries and ages, and has received the sanction of the most applauded writers on the subjects of politics. The opponents of the PLAN proposed have with great assiduity cited and circulated the observations of Montesquieu on the necessity of a contracted territory for a republican government. But they seem not to have been apprised of the sentiments of that great man expressed in another part of his work, nor to have adverted to the consequences of the principle to which they subscribe with such ready acquiescence.

When Montesquieu recommends a small extent for republics, the standards he had in view were of dimensions far short of the limits of almost every one of these States. Neither Virginia, Massachusetts, Pennsylvania, New York, North Carolina, nor Georgia, can by any means be compared with the models from which he reasoned and to which the terms of his description apply. If we therefore take his ideas on this point as the criterion of truth, we shall be driven to the alternative, either of taking refuge at once in the arms of monarchy, or of splitting ourselves into an infinity of little, jealous, clashing, tumultuous commonwealths; the wretched nurseries of unceasing discord and the miserable objects of universal pity or contempt. Some of the writers who have come forward on the other side of the question, seem to have been aware of the dilemma, and have even been bold enough to hint at the division of the larger States as a desirable thing. Such an infatuated policy, such a desperate expedient might, by the multiplication of petty offices, answer the views of men who possess not qualifications to extend their influence beyond the narrow circles of personal intrigue, but it could never promote the greatness or happiness of the people of America. (No. 9)

So FAR ARE the suggestions of Montesquieu from standing in opposition to a general Union of the States, that he explicitly treats of a CONFEDERATE REPUBLIC as the expedient for extending the sphere of popular government and reconciling the advantages of monarchy with those of republicanism. (No. 9)

AMONG THE numerous advantages promised by a well constructed Union, none deserves to be more accurately developed than its tendency to break and control the violence of faction. The friend of popular governments never finds himself so much alarmed for their character and fate, as when he contemplates their propensity to this dangerous vice. He will not fail therefore to set a due value on any plan which, without violating the principles to which he is attached, provides a proper cure for it. The instability, injustice, and confusion introduced into the public councils have in truth been the mortal diseases under which popular governments have every where perished; as they continue to be the favorite and fruitful topics from which the adversaries to liberty derive their most specious declamations. The valuable improvements made by the America Constitutions on the popular models, both ancient and modern, cannot certainly be too much admired. But it would be an unwarrantable partiality to contend that they have as effectually obviated the danger on this side as was wished and expected. Complaints are everywhere heard from our most considerate and virtuous citizens, equally the friends of public and private faith, and of public and personal liberty, that our governments are too unstable; that the public good is disregarded in the conflicts of rival parties; and that measures are too often decided, not according to the rules of justice and the rights of the minor party, but by the superior force of an interested and overbearing majority. However anxiously we may wish that these complaints had no foundation, the evidence of known facts will not permit us to deny that they are in some degree true. It will be found indeed, on a candid review of our situation, that some of the distresses under which we labor have been erroneously charged on the operation of our governments. But it will be found at the same time, that other causes will not alone account for many of our heaviest misfortunes; and particularly, for that prevailing and increasing distrust of public engagements and alarm for private rights which are echoed from one end of the continent to the other. These must be chiefly, if not wholly, effects of the unsteadiness and injustice with which a factious spirit has tainted our public administrations.

By a faction I understand a number of citizens, whether amounting to a majority or minority of the whole, who are united and actuated by some common impulse of passion, or of interest adverse to the rights of other citizens, or to the permanent and aggregate interests of the community.

There are two methods of curing the mischiefs of faction: the one, by removing its causes; the other, by controlling its effects.

There are again two methods of removing the causes of faction: the one, by destroying the liberty which is essential to its existence; the other, by giving to every citizen the same opinions, the same passions, and the same interests.

It could never be more truly said than of the first remedy, that it is worse than the disease. Liberty is to faction what air is to fire, an element without which it instantly expires. But it could not be a less[er] folly to abolish liberty, which is essential to political life, because it nourishes faction, than it would be to wish the annihilation of air, which is essential to animal life, because it imparts to fire its destructive agency.

The second expedient is as impracticable as the first would be unwise. As long as the reason of man continues fallible and he is at liberty to exercise it, different opinions will be formed. As long as the connection subsists between his reason and his self-love, his opinions and his passions will have a reciprocal influence on each other, and the former will be objects to which the latter will attach themselves. The diversity in the faculties of men from which the rights of property originate, is not less an insuperable obstacle to a uniformity of interests. The protection of these faculties is the first object of Government. From the protection of different and unequal faculties of acquiring property, the possession of different degrees and kinds of property immediately results. And from the influence of these on the sentiments and views of the respective proprietors, ensues a division of the society into different interests and parties.

The latent causes of faction are thus sown in the nature of man, and we see them everywhere brought into different degrees of activity, according to the different circumstances of civil society. A zeal for different opinions concerning religion, concerning Government and many other points, as well of speculation as of practice; an attachment to different leaders ambitiously contending for preeminence and power, or to persons of other descriptions whose fortunes have been interesting to the human passions, have in turn divided mankind into parties, inflamed them with mutual animosity, and rendered them much more disposed to vex and oppress each other, than to cooperate for their common good. So strong is this propensity of mankind to fall into mutual animosities, that where no substantial occasion presents itself, the most frivolous and fanciful distinctions have been sufficient to kindle their unfriendly passions, and excite their most violent conflicts. But the most common and durable source of factions has been the various and unequal distribution of property. Those who hold, and those who are without property, have ever formed distinct interests in society. Those who are creditors, and those who are debtors, fall under a like discrimination. A landed interest, a manufacturing interest, a mercantile interest, a monied interest, with many lesser interests, grow up of necessity in civilized nations, and divide them into different classes, actuated by different sentiments and views. The regulation of these various and interfering interests forms the principal task of modern Legislation, and involves the spirit of party and faction in the necessary and ordinary operations of Government.

No man is allowed to be a judge in his own cause, because his interest would certainly bias his judgment, and, not improbably, corrupt his integrity. With equal, nay with greater reason, a body of men are unfit to be both judges and parties at the same time. Yet what are many of the most important acts of legislation, but so many judicial determinations, not indeed concerning the rights of single persons, but concerning the rights of large bodies of citizens; and what are the different classes of legislators, but advocates and parties to the causes which they determine? Is a law proposed concerning private debts? It is a question to which the creditors are parties on one side, and the debtors on the other. Justice ought to hold the balance between them. Yet the parties are and must be themselves the judges; and the most numerous party, or in other words, the most powerful faction must be expected to prevail. Shall domestic manufactures be encouraged, and in what degree, by restrictions on foreign manufactures? are questions which would be differently decided by the landed and the manufacturing classes; and probably by neither with a sole regard to justice and the public good. The apportionment of taxes on the various descriptions of property is an act which seems to require the most exact impartiality; yet there is perhaps no legislative act in which greater opportunity and temptation are given to a predominant party to trample on the rules of justice. Every shilling with which they overburden the inferior number is a shilling saved to their own pockets.

It is in vain to say that enlightened statesmen will be able to adjust these clashing interests, and render them all subservient to the public good. Enlightened statesmen will not always be at the helm. Nor, in many cases, can such an adjustment be made at all without taking into view indirect and remote considerations, which will rarely prevail over the immediate interest which one party may find in disregarding the rights of another or the good of the whole.

The inference to which we are brought is that the *causes* of faction cannot be removed, and that relief is only to be sought in the means of controlling its *effects*.

If a faction consists of less than a majority, relief is supplied by the republican principle, which enables the majority to defeat its sinister views by regular vote. It may clog the administration, it may convulse the society, but it will be unable to execute and mask its violence under the forms of the Constitution. When a majority is included in a faction, the form of popular government on the other hand enables it to sacrifice to its ruling passion or interest, both the public good and the rights of other citizens. To secure the public good and private rights against the danger of such a faction, and at the same time to preserve the spirit and the form of popular government, is then the great object to which our enquiries are directed. Let me add that it is the great desideratum, by which alone this form of government can be rescued from the opprobrium under which it has so long labored, and be recommended to the esteem and adoption of mankind.

By what means is this object attainable? Evidently by one of two only. Either the existence of the same passion or interest in a majority at the same time must be prevented, or the majority, having such coexistent passion or interest, must be rendered by their number and local situation, unable to concert and carry into effect schemes of oppression. If the impulse and the opportunity be suffered to coincide, we well know that neither moral nor religious motives can be relied on as an adequate control. They are not found to be such on the injustice and violence of individuals, and lose their efficacy in proportion to the number combined together; that is, in proportion as their efficacy becomes needful.

From this view of the subject, it may be concluded that a pure Democracy, by which I mean a society consisting of a small number of citizens who assemble and administer the Government in person, can admit of no cure for the mischiefs of faction. A common passion or interest will, in almost every case, be felt by a majority of the whole; a communication and concert results from the form of Government itself; and there is nothing to check the inducements to sacrifice the weaker party or an obnoxious individual. Hence it is that such Democracies have ever been spectacles of turbulence and contention; have ever been found incompatible with personal security or the rights of property; and have in general been as short in their lives, as they have been violent in their deaths. Theoretic politicians who have patronized this species of Government have erroneously supposed that by reducing mankind to a perfect equality in their political rights, they would at the same time be perfectly equalized and assimilated in their possessions, their opinions, and their passions.

A Republic, by which I mean a Government in which the scheme of representation takes place, opens a different prospect, and promises the cure for which we are seeking. Let us examine the points in which it varies from pure Democracy, and we shall comprehend both the nature of the cure, and the efficacy which it must derive from the Union.

The two great points of difference between a Democracy and a Republic are, first, the delegation of the Government, in the latter, to a small number of citizens elected by the rest; secondly, the greater number of citizens, and greater sphere of country, over which the latter may be extended.

The effect of the first difference is, on the one hand, to refine and enlarge the public views by passing them through the medium of a chosen body of citizens whose wisdom may best discern the true interest of their country, and whose patriotism and love of justice will be least likely to sacrifice it to temporary or partial considerations. Under such a regulation it may well happen that the public voice pronounced by the representatives of the people will be more consonant to the public good, than if pronounced by the people themselves convened for the purpose. On the other hand, the effect may be inverted. Men of factious tempers, of local prejudices, or of sinister designs may by intrigue, by corruption, or by other means, first obtain the suffrages, and then betray the interests of the people. The question resulting is whether small or extensive Republics are most favorable to the election of proper guardians of the public weal: and it is clearly decided in favor of the latter by two obvious considerations.

In the first place it is to be remarked that however small the Republic may be, the Representatives must be raised to a certain number in order to guard against the cabals of a few; and that however large it may be, they must be limited to a certain number in order to guard against the confusion of a multitude. Hence the number of Representatives in the two cases, not being in proportion to that of the Constituents, and being proportionally greatest in a small Republic, it follows that if the proportion of fit characters be not less in the large than in the small Republic, the former will present a greater option, and consequently a greater probability of a fit choice.

In the next place, as each Representative will be chosen by a greater number of citizens in the large than in the small Republic, it will be more difficult for unworthy candidates to practice with success the vicious arts by which elections are too often carried; and the suffrages of the people being more free, will be more likely to center on men who possess the most attractive merit, and the most diffusive and established characters.

It must be confessed that in this, as in most other cases, there is a mean on both sides of which inconveniences will be found to lie. By enlarging too much the number of electors, you render the representative too little acquainted with all their local circumstances and lesser interests; as by reducing it too much, you render him unduly attached to these and too little fit to comprehend and pursue great and national objects. The Federal Constitution forms a happy combination in this respect; the great and aggregate interests being referred to the national, the local and particular, to the state legislatures.

The other point of difference is, the greater number of citizens and extent of territory which may be brought within the compass of Republican, than of Democratic Government; and it is this circumstance principally which renders factious combinations less to be dreaded in the former, than in the latter. The smaller the society, the fewer probably will be the distinct parties and interests composing it; the fewer the distinct parties and interests, the more frequently will a majority be found of the same party; and the smaller the number of individuals composing a majority, and the smaller the compass within which they are placed, the more easily will they concert and execute their plans of oppression. Extend the sphere, and you take in a greater variety of parties and interests; you make it less probable that a majority of the whole will have a common motive to invade the rights of other citizens; or if such a common motive exists, it will be more difficult for all who feel it to discover their own strength, and to act in unison with each other. Besides other impediments, it may be remarked that where there is a consciousness of unjust or dishonorable purposes, communication is always checked by distrust in proportion to the number whose concurrence is necessary.

Hence it clearly appears that the same advantage which a Republic has over a Democracy in controlling the effects of faction is enjoyed by a large over a small Republic—is enjoyed by the Union over the States composing it. Does this advantage consist in the substitution of Representatives, whose enlightened views and virtuous sentiments render them superior to local prejudices and to schemes of injustice? It will not be denied that the Representation of the Union will be most likely to possess these requisite endowments. Does it consist in the greater security afforded by a greater variety of parties against the event of any one party being able to outnumber and oppress the rest? In an equal degree does the increased variety of parties comprised within the Union increase this security. Does it, in fine, consist in the greater obstacles opposed to the concert and accomplishment of the secret wishes of an unjust and interested majority? Here again the extent of the Union gives it the most palpable advantage.

The influence of factious leaders may kindle a flame within their particular States, but will be unable to spread a general conflagration through the other States; a religious sect may degenerate into a political faction in a part of the Confederacy; but the variety of sects dispersed over the entire face of it must secure the national Councils against any danger from that source; a rage for paper money, for an abolition of debts, for an equal division of property, or for any other improper or wicked project, will be less apt to pervade the whole body of the Union than a particular member of it; in the same proportion as such a malady is more likely to taint a particular county or district than an entire State.

In the extent and proper structure of the Union, therefore, we behold a Republican remedy for the diseases most incident to Republican Government. And according to the degree of pleasure and pride we feel in being Republicans, ought to be our zeal in cherishing the spirit, and supporting the character of Federalists. (No. 10)

IF EUROPE has the merit of discovering this great mechanical power in government [representation], by the simple agency of which the will of the largest political body may be concentered, and its force directed to any object which the public good requires; America can claim the merit of making the discovery the basis of unmixed and extensive republics. (No. 14)

AS THE NATURAL limit of a democracy is that distance from the central point which will just permit the most remote citizens to assemble as often as their public functions demand, and will include no greater number than can join in those functions; so the natural limit of a republic is that distance from the center which will barely allow the representatives of the people to meet as often as may be necessary for the administration of public affairs. (No. 14)

THE NATURAL CURE for an ill administration in a popular or representative constitution is a change of men. (No. 21)

[T]HE SPIRIT OF PARTY, in different degrees, must be expected to infect all political bodies. (No. 26)

WHERE IN THE name of common sense are our fears to end if we may not trust our sons, our brothers, our neighbors, our fellow-citizens [to represent us]? What shadow of danger can there be from men who are daily mingling with the rest of their countrymen, and who participate with them in the same feelings, sentiments, habits, and interests? (No. 29)

THE IDEA OF an actual representation of all classes of the people by persons of each class is altogether visionary. (No. 35)

IF WE TAKE INTO account the momentary humors or dispositions which may happen to prevail in particular parts of the society, and to which a wise administration will never be inattentive, is the man whose situation leads to extensive inquiry and information less likely to be a competent judge of their nature, extent, and foundation than one whose observation does not travel beyond the circle of his neighbors and acquaintances? Is it not natural that a man who is a candidate for the favor of the people and who is dependent on the suffrages of his fellow-citizens for the continuance of his public honors, should take care to inform himself of their dispositions and inclinations and should be willing to allow them their proper degree of influence upon his conduct? This dependence, and the necessity of being bound himself and his posterity by the laws to which he gives his assent, are the true, and they are the strong chords of sympathy between the representatives and the constituent. (No. 35)

[F]ROM THE NATURAL operation of the different interests and views of the various classes of the community, whether the representation of the people be more or less numerous, it will consist almost entirely of proprietors of land, of merchants, and members of the learned professions who will truly represent all those different interests and views. . . . [T]here are exceptions to the rule, but not in sufficient number to influence the general complexion or character of the government. There are strong minds in every walk of life that will rise superior to the disadvantages of situation, and will command the tribute due to their merit, not only from the classes to which they particularly belong, but from the society in general. The door ought to be equally open to all; and I trust, for the credit of human nature, that we shall see examples of such vigorous plants flourishing in the soil of Federal, as well as of State Legislation; but occasional instances of this sort will not render the reasoning founded upon the general course of things less conclusive. (No. 36)

As TO POLL taxes, I, without scruple, confess my disapprobation to them. . . . I should lament to see them introduced into practice under the national government. (No. 36)

IT IS EVIDENT that no other form [of government but a republican one] would be reconcilable with the genius of the people of America, with the fundamental principles of the revolution, or with that honorable deter- mination, which animates every votary of freedom, to rest all our political experiments on the capacity of mankind for self-government. (No. 39)

[W]E MAY DEFINE a republic to be . . . a government which derives all its powers directly or indirectly from the great body of the people, and is administered by persons holding their offices during pleasure, for a lim- ited period, or during good behavior. It is *essential* to such a government that it be derived from the great body of the society, not from an incon- siderable proportion or a favored class of it. . . . It is *sufficient* for such a government, that the persons administering it be appointed, either di- rectly or indirectly, by the people, and that they hold their appointments by either of the tenures just specified. Otherwise every government in the United States, as well as every other popular government that has been or can be well executed, would be degraded from the republican character. (No. 39)

WITHOUT THE *substance* of this power ["necessary and proper" clause], the whole Constitution would be a dead letter. (No. 44)

THE FOUNDERS OF our republics have so much merit for the wisdom which they have displayed, that no task can be less pleasing than that of point- ing out the errors into which they have fallen. A respect for truth, however, obliges us to remark that they seem never for a moment to have turned their eyes from the danger to liberty from the overgrown and all-grasp- ing prerogative of an hereditary magistrate, supported and fortified by an hereditary branch of the legislative authority. They seem never to have recollected the danger from legislative usurpations which, by as- sembling all power in the same hands, must lead to the same tyranny as is threatened by executive usurpations.

    In a government where numerous and extensive prerogatives are placed in the hands of a hereditary monarch, the executive department is very justly regarded as the source of danger, and watched with all the jealousy which a zeal for liberty ought to inspire. In a democracy, where a multitude of people exercise in person the legislative functions, and are continually exposed by their incapacity for regular deliberation and concerted measures to the ambitious intrigues of their executive magistrates, tyranny may well be apprehended on some favorable emergency to start up in the same quarter. But in a representative republic, where the executive magistracy is carefully limited both in the extent and the duration of its power; and where the legislative power is exercised by an assembly, which is inspired by a supposed influence over the people with an intrepid confidence in its own strength; which is sufficiently numerous to feel all the passions which actuate a multitude; yet not so numerous as to be incapable of pursuing the objects of its passions by means which reason prescribes; it is against the enterprising ambition of this department, that the people ought to indulge all their jealousy and exhaust all their precautions.

The legislative department derives a superiority in our governments from other circumstances. Its constitutional powers being at once more extensive and less susceptible of precise limits, it can with greater facility mask under complicated and indirect measures, the encroachments which it makes on the co-ordinate departments. It is not infrequently a question of real nicety in legislative bodies, whether the operation of a particular measure will or will not extend beyond the legislative sphere. On the other side, the executive power being restrained within a narrower compass, and being more simple in its nature; and the judiciary being described by landmarks still less uncertain, projects of usurpation by either of these departments would immediately betray and defeat themselves. Nor is this all: As the legislative department alone has access to the pockets of the people, and has in some constitutions full discretion, and in all a prevailing influence over the pecuniary rewards of those who fill the other departments, a dependence is thus created in the latter which gives still greater facility to encroachments of the former. (No. 48)

THE DEFINITION OF the right of suffrage is very justly regarded as a fundamental article of republican government. It was incumbent on the Convention therefore to define and establish this right in the Constitution. To have left it open for the occasional regulation of the Congress would have been improper for the reason just mentioned. To have submitted it to the legislative discretion of the States would have been improper for the same reason; and for the additional reason that it would have rendered too dependent on the State Governments that branch of the Federal Government which ought to be dependent on the people alone. To have reduced the different qualifications in the different States to one uniform rule would probably have been as unsatisfactory to some of the States, as it would have been difficult to the Convention. The provision made by the Convention appears, therefore, to be the best that lay within their option. It must be satisfactory to every State, because it is conformable to the standard already established, or which may be established by the State itself. It will be safe to the United States, because, being fixed by the State Constitutions it is not alterable by the State Governments, and it cannot be feared that the people of the States will alter this part of their constitutions in such a manner as to abridge the rights secured to them by the Federal Constitution. (No. 52)

As IT IS ESSENTIAL to liberty that the government, in general, should have a common interest with the people; so it is particularly essential that the branch of it under consideration [House of Representatives] should have an immediate dependence on, and an intimate sympathy with the people. Frequent elections are unquestionably the only policy by which this dependence and sympathy can be effectually secured. (No. 52)

[IN THE FIRST PLACE] the Federal Legislature will possess a part only of that supreme legislative authority which is vested completely in the British parliament, and which with few exceptions was exercised by the colonial assemblies and the Irish legislature. It is a received and well founded maxim that where no other circumstances affect the case, the greater the power is, the shorter ought to be its duration; and, conversely, the smaller the power, the more safely may its duration be protracted. In the second place, it has on another occasion been shown that the Federal Legislature will not only be restrained by its dependence on the people as other legislative bodies are; but that it will be moreover watched and controlled by the several collateral [state] Legislatures, which other legislative bodies are not. And in the third place, no comparison can be made between the means that will be possessed by the more permanent branches of the Federal Government for seducing, if they should be disposed to seduce, the House of Representatives from their duty to the people, and the means of influence over the popular branch, possessed by the other branches of the government above cited. With less power therefore to abuse, the Federal Representatives can be less tempted on one side, and will be doubly watched on the other. (No. 52)

THE IMPORTANT distinction so well understood in America between a constitution established by the people, and unalterable by the government, and a law established by the government, and alterable by the government, seems to have been little understood and less observed in any other country. Wherever the supreme power of legislation has resided, has been supposed to reside also a full power to change the form of the government. Even in Great Britain, where the principles of political and civil liberty have been most discussed, and where we hear most of the rights of the [English] Constitution, it is maintained that the authority of the Parliament is transcendent and uncontrollable, as well with regard to the constitution, as the ordinary objects of legislative provision. They have accordingly, in several instances, actually changed by legislative acts some of the most fundamental articles of the government. They have in particular, on several occasions, changed the periods of election; and on the last occasion, not only introduced septennial, in the place of triennial, elections, but by the same act continued themselves in place four years beyond the term for which they were elected by the people. An attention to these dangerous practices has produced a very natural alarm in the votaries of free government, of which frequency of elections is the cornerstone; and has led them to seek for some security to liberty against the danger to which it is exposed. Where no constitution paramount to the government either existed or could be obtained, no constitutional security similar to that established in the United States was to be attempted. Some other security, therefore, was to be sought for; and what better security would the case admit than that of selecting and appealing to some simple and familiar portion of time as a standard for measuring the danger of innovations, for fixing the national sentiment, and for uniting the patriotic exertions. The most simple and familiar portion of time applicable to the subject was that of a year; and hence the doctrine has been inculcated by a laudable zeal to erect some barrier against the gradual innovations of an unlimited government, that the advance towards tyranny was to be calculated by the distance of departure from the fixed point of annual elections. But what necessity can there be of applying this expedient to a government, limited as the federal government will be, by the authority of a paramount constitution? Or who will pretend that the liberties of the people of America will not be more secure under biennial elections, unalterably fixed by such a constitution, than those of any other nation would be, where elections were annual or even more frequent, but subject to alterations by the ordinary power of the government? . . .

No man can be a competent legislator who does not add to an upright intention and a sound judgment, a certain degree of knowledge of the subjects on which he is to legislate. A part of this knowledge may be acquired by means of information which lie within the compass of men in private as well as public stations. Another part can only be attained, or at least thoroughly attained, by actual experience in the station which requires the use of it. The period of service ought, therefore, in all such cases, to bear some proportion to the extent of practical knowledge requisite to the due performance of the service. (No. 53)

IN A SINGLE STATE the requisite knowledge relates to the existing laws which are uniform throughout the state, and with which all the citizens are more or less conversant; and to the general affairs of the state, which lie within a small compass are not very diversified, and occupy much of the attention and conversation of every class of people. The great theater of the United States presents a very different scene. The laws are so far from being uniform that they vary in every state; whilst the public affairs of the union are spread throughout a very extensive region, and are extremely diversified by the local affairs connected with them, and can with difficulty be correctly learnt in any other place than in the central councils, to which a knowledge of them will be brought by the representatives of every part of the empire. Yet some knowledge of the affairs, and even of the laws of all the states, ought to be possessed by the members from each of the states. How can foreign trade be properly regulated by uniform laws without some acquaintance with the commerce, the ports, the usages, and the regulations of the different states? How can the trade between the different states be duly regulated without some knowledge of their relative situations in these and other points? How can taxes be judiciously imposed and effectually collected if they be not accommodated to the different laws and local circumstances relating to these objects in the different states? How can uniform regulations for the militia be duly provided without a similar knowledge of some internal circumstances by which the states are distinguished from each other? These are the principal objects of federal legislation, and suggest most forcibly the extensive information which the representatives ought to acquire. The other inferior objects will require a proportional degree of information with regard to them.

It is true that all these difficulties will by degrees be very much diminished. The most laborious task will be the proper inauguration of the government and the primeval formation of a federal code. Improvements on the first draft will every year become both easier and fewer. Past transactions of the government will be a ready and accurate source of information to new members. The affairs of the union will become more and more objects of curiosity and conversation among the citizens at large. And the increased intercourse among those of different states will contribute not a little to diffuse a mutual knowledge of their affairs, as this again will contribute to a general assimilation of their manners and laws. But with all these abatements the business of federal legislation must continue so far to exceed both in novelty and difficulty the legislative business of a single state, as to justify the longer period of service assigned to those who are to transact it. (No. 53)

A FEW OF THE members [of the House of Representatives], as happens in all assemblies, will possess superior talents, will by frequent re-elections become members of long standing, will be thoroughly masters of the public business, and perhaps not unwilling to avail themselves of those advantages. The greater the proportion of new members, and the less the information of the bulk of the members, the more apt will they be to fall into the snares that may be laid for them. (No. 53)

IN GENERAL IT may be remarked . . . that no political problem is less susceptible of a precise solution than that which relates to the number most convenient for a representative legislature. (No. 55)

[T]HE RATIO between the representatives and the people ought not to be the same where the latter are very numerous, as where they are very few. (No. 55)

SIXTY OR SEVENTY men may be more properly trusted with a given degree of power than six or seven. But it does not follow that six or seven hundred would be proportionally a better depository. And if we carry on the supposition to six or seven thousand the whole reasoning ought to be reversed. The truth is that in all cases a certain number at least seems to be necessary to secure the benefits of free consultation and discussion, and to guard against too easy a combination for improper purposes. As on the other hand, the number ought at most to be kept within a certain limit in order to avoid the confusion and intemperance of a multitude. In all very numerous assemblies of whatever characters composed, passion never fails to wrest the scepter from reason. Had every Athenian citizen been a Socrates, every Athenian assembly would still have been a mob. (No. 55)

As THERE IS a degree of depravity in mankind which requires a certain degree of circumspection and distrust, so there are other qualities in human nature which justify a certain portion of esteem and confidence. Republican government presupposes the existence of these [latter] qualities in a higher degree than any other form. Were the pictures which have been drawn by the political jealousy of some among us faithful likenesses of the human character, the inference would be that there is not sufficient virtue among men for self-government, and that nothing less than the chains of despotism can restrain them from destroying and devouring one another. (No. 55)

IT IS A SOUND and important principle that the representative ought to be acquainted with the interests and circumstances of his constituents. But this principle can extend no farther than to those circumstances and interests to which the authority and care of the representative relate. An ignorance of a variety of minute and particular objects which do not lie within the compass of legislation is consistent with every attribute necessary to a due performance of the legislative trust. In determining the extent of information required in the exercise of a particular authority, recourse then must be had to the objects within the purview of that authority. (No. 56)

THE AIM of every political constitution is, or ought to be, first, to obtain for rulers men who possess most wisdom to discern, and most virtue to pursue the common good of the society; and in the next place, to take the most effectual precautions for keeping them virtuous whilst they continue to hold their public trust. The elective mode of obtaining rulers is the characteristic policy of republican government. The means relied on in this form of government for preventing their degeneracy are numerous and various. The most effectual one is such a limitation of the term of appointments as will maintain a proper responsibility to the people. (No. 57)

WHO ARE TO be the objects of [the electorate's] popular choice? Every citizen whose merit may recommend him to the esteem and confidence of his country. No qualification of wealth, of birth, of religious faith, or of civil profession is permitted to fetter the judgment or disappoint the inclination of the people.

If we consider the situation of the men on whom the free suffrages of their fellow citizens may confer the representative trust, we shall find it involving every security which can be devised or desired for their fidelity to their constituents.

In the first place, as they will have been distinguished by the preference of their fellow citizens, we are to presume that in general they will be somewhat distinguished also by those qualities which entitle them to it, and which promise a sincere and scrupulous regard to the nature of their engagements.

In the second place, they will enter into the public service under circumstances which cannot fail to produce a temporary affection at least to their constituents. There is in every breast a sensibility to marks of honor, of favor, of esteem, and of confidence which, apart from all considerations of interest, is some pledge for grateful and benevolent returns. Ingratitude is a common topic of declamation against human nature;

and it must be confessed that instances of it are but too frequent and flagrant both in public and in private life. But the universal and extreme indignation which it inspires is itself a proof of the energy and prevalence of the contrary sentiment.

In the third place, these ties which bind the representative to his constituents are strengthened by motives of a more selfish nature. His pride and vanity attach him to a form of government which favors his pretensions, and gives him a share in its honors and distinctions. Whatever hopes or projects might be entertained by a few aspiring characters, it must generally happen that a great proportion of the men deriving their advancement from their influence with the people would have more to hope from a preservation of the favor, than from innovations in the government subversive of the authority of the people.

All these securities, however, would be found very insufficient without the restraint of frequent elections. Hence, in the fourth place, the House of Representatives is so constituted as to support in the members a habitual recollection of their dependence on the people. Before the sentiments impressed on their minds by the mode of their elevation can be effaced by the exercise of power, they will be compelled to anticipate the moment when their power is to cease, when their exercise of it is to be reviewed, and when they must descend to the level from which they were raised; there forever to remain, unless a faithful discharge of their trust shall have established their title to a renewal of it.

I will add as a fifth circumstance in the situation of the House of Representatives, restraining them from oppressive measures, that they can make no law which will not have its full operation on themselves and their friends, as well as on the great mass of the society. This has always been deemed one of the strongest bonds by which human policy can connect the rulers and the people together. It creates between them that communion of interests and sympathy of sentiments of which few governments have furnished examples, but without which every government degenerates into tyranny. If it be asked, what is to restrain the House of Representatives from making legal discriminations in favor of themselves and a particular class of the society? I answer, the genius of the whole system, the nature of just and constitutional laws, and above all, the vigilant and manly spirit which actuates the people of America, a spirit which nourishes freedom, and in return is nourished by it.

If this spirit shall ever be so far debased as to tolerate a law not obligatory on the Legislature as well as on the people, the people will be prepared to tolerate anything but liberty.

Such will be the relation between the House of Representatives and their constituents. Duty, gratitude, interest, ambition itself, are the chords by which they will be bound to fidelity and sympathy with the great mass of the people. It is possible that these may all be insufficient to control the caprice and wickedness of man. But are they not all that government will admit, and that human prudence can devise? Are they not the genuine and the characteristic means by which Republican Government provides for the liberty and happiness of the people? Are they not the identical means on which every State Government in the Union relies for the attainment of these important ends? (No. 57)

[THE] POWER OVER the purse may in fact be regarded as the most complete and effectual weapon with which any constitution can arm the immediate representatives of the people for obtaining a redress of every grievance, and for carrying into effect every just and salutary measure. (No. 58)

[I]N ALL LEGISLATIVE assemblies, the greater the number composing them may be, the fewer will be the men who will in fact direct their proceedings. In the first place, the more numerous any assembly may be, of whatever characters composed, the greater is known to be the ascendancy of passion over reason. In the next place, the larger the number, the greater will be the proportion of members of limited information and of weak capacities. Now it is precisely on characters of this description that the eloquence and address of the few are known to act with all their force. In the ancient republics, where the whole body of the people assembled in person, a single orator, or an artful statesman, was generally seen to rule with as complete a sway as if a scepter had been placed in his single hands. On the same principle, the more multitudinous a representative assembly may be rendered, the more it will partake of the infirmities incident to collective meetings of the people. Ignorance will be the dupe of cunning, and passion the slave of sophistry and declamation. The people can never err more than in supposing that by multiplying their representatives beyond a certain limit, they strengthen the barrier against the government of a few. Experience will forever admonish them that on the contrary, *after securing a sufficient number for the purposes of safety, of local information, and of diffusive sympathy with the whole society,* they will counteract their own views by every addition to their representatives. The countenance of the government may become more democratic, but the soul that animates it will be more oligarchic. The machine will be enlarged, but the fewer, and often the more secret, will be the springs by which its motions are directed. (No. 58)

THERE IS sufficient diversity in the state of property, in the genius, manners, and habits of the people of the different parts of the union to occasion a material diversity of disposition in their representatives towards the different ranks and conditions in society. And though an intimate intercourse under the same government will promote a gradual assimilation of temper and sentiment, yet there are causes, as well physical as moral, which may in a greater or less degree permanently nourish different propensities and inclinations in this particular. But the circumstance which will be likely to have the greatest influence in the matter will be the dissimilar modes of constituting the several component parts of the government. (No. 60)

IT IS MORE THAN possible that this uniformity [in electing members of Congress] may be found by experience to be of great importance to the public welfare; both as a security against the perpetuation of the same spirit in the body, and as a cure for the diseases of faction. (No. 61)

IT IS A MISFORTUNE incident to republican government, though in a less degree than to other governments, that those who administer it may forget their obligations to their constituents, and prove unfaithful to their important trust. In this point of view, a senate, as a second branch of the legislative assembly, distinct from and dividing the power with a first, must be in all cases a salutary check on the government. It doubles the security to the people by requiring the concurrence of two distinct bodies in schemes of usurpation or perfidy, where the ambition or corruption of one would otherwise be sufficient. This is a precaution founded on such clear principles and now so well understood in the United States, that it would be more than superfluous to enlarge on it. I will barely remark that as the improbability of sinister combinations will be in proportion to the dissimilarity in the genius of the two bodies, it must be politic to distinguish them from each other by every circumstance which will consist with a due harmony in all proper measures, and with the genuine principles of republican government. (No. 62)

THE NECESSITY of a senate is not less indicated by the propensity of all single and numerous assemblies to yield to the impulse of sudden and violent passions, and to be seduced by factious leaders into intemperate and pernicious resolutions. Examples on this subject might be cited without number, and from proceedings within the United States, as well as from the history of other nations. But a position that will not be contradicted need not be proved. All that need be remarked is that a body which is to correct this infirmity ought itself be free from it, and consequently ought to be less numerous. It ought moreover to possess great firmness, and consequently ought to hold its authority by a tenure of considerable duration. (No. 62)

RESPONSIBILITY, in order to be reasonable, must be limited to objects within the power of the responsible party; and in order to be effectual, must relate to operations of that power of which a ready and proper judgment can be formed by the constituents. The objects of government may be divided into two general classes: the one depending on measures which have singly an immediate and sensible operation; the other depending on a succession of well chosen and well connected measures which have a gradual and perhaps unobserved operation. The importance of the latter description to the collective and permanent welfare of every country needs no explanation. And yet it is evident that an assembly elected for so short a term as to be unable to provide more than one or two links in a chain of measures on which the general welfare may essentially depend, ought not to be answerable for the final result . . . Nor is it possible for the people to estimate the *share* of influence which their annual assemblies may respectively have on events resulting from the mixed transactions of several years. It is sufficiently difficult, at any rate, to preserve a personal responsibility in the members of a *numerous* body for such acts of the body as have an immediate, detached, and palpable operation on its constituents.

The proper remedy for this defect must be an additional body in the legislative department, which having sufficient permanency to provide for such objects as require a continued attention and a train of measures, may be justly and effectually answerable for the attainment of those objects. . . . I shall not scruple to add that such an institution may be sometimes necessary as a defense to the people against their own temporary errors and delusion. As the cool and deliberate sense of the community ought in all governments, and actually will in all free governments, ultimately prevail over the views of its rulers; so there are particular moments in public affairs when the people, stimulated by some irregular passion, or some illicit advantage, or misled by the artful misrepresentations of interested men, may call for measures which they themselves will afterwards be the most ready to lament and condemn. In these critical moments, how salutary will be the interference of some temperate and respectable body of citizens, in order to check the misguided career, and to suspend the blow meditated by the people against themselves, until reason, justice, and truth can regain their authority over the public mind? What bitter anguish would not the people of Athens have often escaped, if their government had contained so provident a safeguard against the tyranny of their own passions? Popular liberty might then have escaped the indelible reproach of decreeing to the same citizens the hemlock on one day, and statues on the next.

It may be suggested that a people spread over an extensive region cannot, like the crowded inhabitants of a small district, be subject to the infection of violent passions, or to the danger of combining in the pursuit of unjust measures. I am far from denying that this is a distinction of peculiar importance. I have on the contrary endeavored . . . to show that it is one of the principal recommendations of a confederated republic. At the same time this advantage ought not to be considered as superseding the use of auxiliary precautions. . . .

It adds no small weight to all these considerations, to recollect, that history informs us of no long-lived republic which had not a senate. . . . [The examples of Sparta, Rome, and Carthage], though as unfit for imitation as they are repugnant to the genius of America, are notwithstanding, when compared with the fugitive and turbulent existence of other ancient republics, very instructive proofs of the necessity of some institution that will blend stability with liberty. I am not unaware of the circumstances which distinguish the American from other popular governments, as well ancient as modern, and which render extreme circumspection necessary in reasoning from the one case to the other. But after allowing due weight to this consideration, it may still be maintained that there are many points of similitude which render these examples not unworthy of our attention. Many of the defects, as we have seen, which can only be supplied by a senatorial institution, are common to a numerous assembly frequently elected by the people, and to the people themselves. There are others, peculiar to the former, which require the control of such an institution. The people can never wilfully betray their own interests. But they may possibly be betrayed by the representatives of the people; and the danger will be evidently greater where the whole legislative trust is lodged in the hands of one body of men, than where the concurrence of separate and dissimilar bodies is required in every public act.

The difference most relied on between the American and other republics consists in the principle of representation, which is the pivot on which the former move, and which is supposed to have been unknown to the latter, or at least to the ancient part of them. (No. 63)

THE TRUE distinction between [the democracies of the ancient world] and the American Governments lies *in the total exclusion of the people in their collective capacity* from any share in the *latter*, and not in the *total exclusion of the representatives of the people*, from the administration of the *former*. The distinction, however thus qualified, must be admitted to leave a most advantageous superiority in favor of the United States. But to ensure to this advantage its full effect, we must be careful not to separate it from the other advantage of an extensive territory. For it cannot be believed that any form of representative government could have succeeded within the narrow limits occupied by the democracies of Greece. (No. 63)

BY EXCLUDING men under thirty-five from the first office [presidency], and those under thirty from the second [senate], it confines the elections to men of whom the people have had time to form a judgment, and with respect to whom they will not be liable to be deceived by those brilliant appearances of genius and patriotism, which like transient meteors, sometimes mislead as well as dazzle. (No. 64)

EVERY CONSIDERATION that can influence the human mind, such as honor, oaths, reputation, conscience, the love of country, and family affections and attachments, afford security for their [senators'] fidelity. (No. 64)

THERE IS an excess of refinement in the idea of disabling the people to continue in office men who had entitled themselves, in their opinion, to approbation and confidence; the advantages of which are at best speculative and equivocal, and are overbalanced by disadvantages far more certain and decisive. (No. 72)

# 6

---

# The Executive Branch
# and the Presidency

T HE COLONISTS' EXPERIENCE WITH
*officials of the British crown fostered a deep distrust of executive power in America.
This distrust was reflected in the Articles of Confederation (which lacked an
executive branch altogether) and in many of the first state constitutions, which
severely limited executive power and made it dependent upon the legislature.
The inadequacy of this arrangement soon became apparent, and over the next
fifteen years many states revised their constitutions in order to lend strength and
independence to the executive. The demands of war taught Americans the value
of a strong, independent executive; the perils of peace would teach them the
dangers of a preponderant, unchecked legislature.*

*These lessons were fresh in the minds of the framers of the Constitution,
many of whom sought to create an "energetic" executive which, among other
things, was capable of withstanding the "vortex" of legislative power. Others,
however, remained suspicious of an "elected monarch" and sought to curb the
abuse of executive power by such measures as a plural presidency, legislative
election, a non-renewable term, and an advisory council. While the Convention
agreed to a single executive early in its proceedings, the specifics of tenure, powers, and election evaded resolution for the next three months. As Publius later*

wrote, "hardly any part of the [constitutional] system could have been attended with greater difficulty in the arrangement of it" than the executive branch.

The executive's tenure and mode of selection were closely linked in the Convention debates. It was generally agreed that election by the legislature implied a single, non-renewable term of seven to nine years, whereas popular election suggested a shorter, renewable term. Since neither formula was able to gain majority support, the Convention settled on a four-year, renewable term for the "president," and an indirect mode of selection by electors chosen in the states. These electors have come to be known as the electoral college.

Differences of opinion over the powers of the presidency were resolved largely in favor of those who advocated a strong, independent executive. In sum, the Constitution gave the president the power to (1) veto acts of Congress; (2) issue pardons and reprieves; (3) receive ambassadors, (4) convene Congress; and (5) adjourn Congress if the two houses could not agree when to do so. With the "advice and consent" of the Senate, the president could (6) make treaties and (7) appoint judges, ambassadors, and other high federal officers. The executive was also made (8) commander-in-chief of the military and (9) was authorized to call the state militias into national service.

More broadly, the president was responsible for "faithfully" executing the laws of the national government and was bound by oath to "preserve, protect, and defend the Constitution of the United States." To check a president guilty of "Treason, Bribery, or other high Crimes and Misdemeanors," the Convention provided a constitutional means of removing the executive (impeachment and trial) and filling the vacancy (succession of the vice-president) in an orderly manner.

Despite this safeguard, the Constitution's provision for a strong executive was a major point of contention in the ratification debates. In response to critics, Publius (Hamilton) labored to refute the charge that "a vigorous executive is inconsistent with the genius of republican government." Not only was a single, "energetic" executive compatible with republicanism, Hamilton argued, it was "a leading character in the definition of good government." Conversely, a "feeble" or plural executive—one lacking in the capacity for "[d]ecision, activity, secrecy, and dispatch"—was a leading feature of "bad government." To support this view, Hamilton skillfully underscored the dangers of weak and divided counsels, and the indispensability of firm and decisive leadership. In this capacity, Publius not only anticipated the practical character of the first presidency; he also created the theoretical framework for all subsequent discussions of the executive's role in governance and place in the constitutional order.

THERE IS HARDLY any part of the system which could have been attended with greater difficulty in the arrangement of it than [the executive branch]. (No. 67)

TALENTS FOR low intrigue and the little arts of popularity may alone suffice to elevate a man to the first honors in a single state; but it will require other talents and a different kind of merit to establish him in the esteem and confidence of the whole union, or of so considerable a portion of it as would be necessary to make him a successful candidate for the distinguished office of president of the United States. It will not be too strong to say that there will be a constant probability of seeing the station filled by characters preeminent for ability and virtue. (No. 68)

[T]HE PRESIDENT will have only the occasional command of such part of the militia of the nation as by legislative provision may be called into the actual service of the Union. (No. 69)

THERE IS AN IDEA, which is not without its advocates, that a vigorous executive is inconsistent with the genius of republican government. The enlightened well-wishers to this species of government must at least hope that the supposition is destitute of foundation, since they can never admit its truth without at the same time admitting the condemnation of their own principles. Energy in the executive is a leading character in the definition of good government. It is essential to the protection of the community against foreign attacks. It is not less essential to the steady administration of the laws, to the protection of property against those irregular and high-handed combinations which sometimes interrupt the ordinary course of justice, to the security of liberty against the enterprises and assaults of ambition, of faction, and of anarchy. (No. 70)

A FEEBLE EXECUTIVE implies a feeble execution of the government. A feeble execution is but another phrase for a bad execution. And a government ill-executed, whatever it may be in theory, must be in practice a bad government. (No. 70)

THE INGREDIENTS which constitute energy in the executive are, first, unity, secondly duration, thirdly an adequate provision for its support, fourthly competent powers. (No. 70)

THOSE POLITICIANS and statesmen who have been the most celebrated for the soundness of their principles, and for the justness of their views, have declared in favor of a single executive and a numerous legislature. They have with great propriety considered energy as the most necessary qualification of the former, and have regarded this as most applicable to power in a single hand; while they have with equal propriety considered the latter as best adapted to deliberation and wisdom, and best calculated to conciliate the confidence of the people and to secure their privileges and interests.

That unity is conducive to energy will not be disputed. Decision, activity, secrecy, and dispatch will generally characterize the proceedings of one man in a much more eminent degree, than the proceedings of any greater number; and in proportion as the number is increased, these qualities will be diminished. (No. 70)

THE EXPERIENCE of other nations will afford little instruction on this head. As far however as it teaches anything, it teaches us not to be enamored of plurality in the executive. (No. 70)

IN THE LEGISLATURE, promptitude of decision is oftener an evil than a benefit. The differences of opinion, and the jarrings of parties in that department of the government, though they may sometimes obstruct salutary plans, yet often promote deliberation and circumspection, and serve to check the excesses in the majority. When a resolution too is once taken, the opposition must be at an end. That resolution is a law, and resistance to it punishable. But no favorable circumstances palliate or atone for the disadvantages of dissention in the executive department. Here they are pure and unmixed. (No. 70)

MAN, in public trust, will much oftener act in such a manner as to render him unworthy of being any longer trusted, than in such a manner as to make him obnoxious to legal punishment. But the multiplication of the executive adds to the difficulty of detection in either case. (No. 70)

THE IDEA OF a council to the executive, which has so generally obtained in the state constitutions, has been derived from that maxim of republican jealousy which considers power as safer in the hands of a number of men than of a single man. If the maxim should be admitted to be applicable to the case, I should contend that the advantage on that side would not counterbalance the numerous disadvantages on the opposite side. But I do not think the rule at all applicable to the executive power. I clearly concur in the opinion in this particular with a writer whom the celebrated Junius* pronounces to be "deep, solid and ingenious;" that

---

*Junius, *Stat Nominis Umbra* (London, 1772). Junius is refering to Jean Louis de Lolme, author of *The Constitution of England, or An Account of the English Government* ..., 3rd ed. (London, 1781). (Editor)

"the executive power is more easily confined when it is one;" that it is far more safe there should be a single object for the jealousy and watchfulness of the people; and in a word, that all multiplication of the executive is rather dangerous than friendly to liberty. (No. 70)

WHEN [EXECUTIVE] power . . . is placed in the hands of so small a number of men as to admit of their interests and views being easily combined in a common enterprise by an artful leader, it becomes more liable to abuse and more dangerous when abused, than if it be lodged in the hands of one man, who from the very circumstance of his being alone will be more narrowly watched and more readily suspected, and who cannot unite so great a mass of influence as when he is associated with others. (No. 70)

A COUNCIL to a magistrate, who is himself responsible for what he does, are generally nothing better than a clog upon his good intentions, are often the instruments and accomplices of his bad [ones], and are almost always a cloak to his faults. (No. 70)

THERE ARE some who would be inclined to regard the servile pliancy of the executive to a prevailing current, either in the community or in the Legislature, as its best recommendation. But such men entertain very crude notions, as well of the purposes for which government was instituted, as of the true means by which the public happiness may be promoted. The republican principle demands that the deliberate sense of the community should govern the conduct of those to whom they entrust the management of their affairs; but it does not require an unqualified complaisance to every sudden breeze of passion, or to every transient impulse which the people may receive from the arts of men who flatter their prejudices to betray their interests. It is a just observation that the people commonly *intend* the PUBLIC GOOD. This often applies to their very errors. But their good sense would despise the adulator who should pretend that they always *reason right* about the *means* of promoting it. They know from experience that they sometimes err; and the wonder is that they so seldom err as they do, beset as they continually are by the wiles of parasites and sycophants, by the snares of the ambitious, the avaricious, the desperate; by the artifices of men who possess their confidence more than they deserve it; and of those who seek to possess, rather than to deserve it. When occasions present themselves in which the interests of the people are at variance with their inclinations, it is the duty of the persons whom they have appointed to be the guardians of those interests to withstand the temporary delusion in order to give them time and opportunity for more cool and sedate reflection. Instances might be cited in which a conduct of this kind has saved the people from very fatal consequences of their own mistakes, and has procured lasting monuments of their gratitude to the men who had courage and magnanimity enough to serve them at the peril of their displeasure. (No. 71)

THE ADMINISTRATION of government, in its largest sense, comprehends all the operations of the body politic, whether legislative, executive, or judicial; but in its most usual and perhaps in its most precise signification, it is limited to executive details, and falls peculiarly within the province of the executive department. The actual conduct of foreign negotiations, the preparatory plans of finance, the application and disbursement of the public monies in conformity to the general appropriations of the legislature; the arrangement of the army and navy, the direction of the operations of war; these and other matters of a like nature constitute what seems to be most properly understood by the administration of government. The persons, therefore, to whose immediate management these different matters are committed, ought to be considered as the assistants or deputies of the chief magistrate; and, on this account, they ought to derive their offices from his appointment, at least from his nomination, and ought to be subject to his superintendence. This view of the subject will at once suggest to us the intimate connection between the duration of the executive magistrate in office, and the stability of the system of administration. To reverse and undo what has been done by a predecessor is very often considered by a successor as the best proof he can give of his own capacity and desert, and in addition to this propensity, where the alteration has been the result of pubic choice, the person substituted is warranted in supposing that the dismissal of his predecessor has proceeded from a dislike of his measures, and that the less he resembles him the more he will recommend himself to the favor of his constituents. These considerations, and the influence of personal confidences and attachments, would be likely to induce every new president to promote a change of men to fill the subordinate stations; and these causes together could not fail to occasion a disgraceful and ruinous mutability in the administration of the government. (No. 72)

THERE ARE FEW men who would not feel much less zeal in the discharge of a duty, when they were conscious that the advantages of the station with which it was connected must be relinquished at a determinate period, than when they were permitted to entertain a hope of *obtaining* by *meriting* a continuance of them. This position will not be disputed so long as it is admitted that the desire of reward is one of the strongest incentives of human conduct, or that the best security for the fidelity of mankind is to make their interest coincide with their duty. Even the love of fame, the ruling passion of the noblest minds, which would prompt a man to plan and undertake extensive and arduous enterprises for the public benefit, requiring considerable time to mature and perfect them; if he could flatter himself with the prospect of being allowed to finish what he had begun, would on the contrary deter him from the undertaking, when he foresaw that he must quit the scene before he could accomplish the work, and must commit that, together with his own reputation, to hands which might be unequal or unfriendly to the task. The most to be expected from the generality of men in such a situation, is the negative merit of not doing harm instead of the positive merit of doing good. (No. 72)

THAT EXPERIENCE is the parent of wisdom is an adage, the truth of which is recognized by the wisest as well as the simplest of mankind. What [could be] more desirable or more essential than this quality in the governors of nations? What more desirable or more essential than in the first magistrate of a nation? (No. 72)

THERE IS NO nation which has not at one period or another experienced an absolute necessity of the services of particular men, in particular situations; perhaps it would not be too strong to say, to the preservation of its political existence. How unwise therefore must be every such self-denying ordinance, as serves to prohibit a nation from making use of its own citizens in the manner best suited to its exigencies and circumstances! Without supposing the personal essentiality of the man, it is evident that a change of the chief magistrate at the breaking out of a war, or at any similar crisis, for another even of equal merit, would at all times be detrimental to the community; inasmuch as it would substitute inexperience to experience and would tend to unhinge and set afloat the already settled train of the administration. (No. 72)

THERE ARE MEN who could neither be distressed nor won into a sacrifice of their duty; but this stern virtue is the growth of few soils. And in the main, it will be found that a power over a man's support is a power over his will. If it were necessary to confirm so plain a truth by facts, examples would not be wanting, even in this country, of the intimidation or seduction of the executive by the terrors or allurements of the pecuniary arrangements of the legislative body. (No. 73)

OF ALL THE cares or concerns of government, the direction of war most peculiarly demands those qualities which distinguish the exercise of power by a single hand. The direction of war implies the direction of the common strength; and the power of directing and employing the common strength forms an usual and essential part in the definition of the executive authority. (No. 74)

HUMANITY AND GOOD policy conspire to dictate that the benign prerogative of pardoning should be as little as possible fettered or embarrassed. The criminal code of every country partakes so much of necessary severity that without an easy access to exceptions in favor of unfortunate guilt, justice would wear a countenance too sanguinary and cruel. As the sense of responsibility is always strongest in proportion as it is undivided, it may be inferred that a single man would be most ready to attend to the force of those motives which might plead for a mitigation of the rigor of the law, and least apt to yield to considerations which were calculated to shelter a fit object of its vengeance. The reflection, that the fate of a fellow creature depended on his *sole fiat*, would naturally inspire scrupulousness and caution. The dread of being accused of weakness or connivance would beget equal circumspection, though of a different kind. On the other hand, as men generally derive confidence from their numbers, they might often encourage each other in an act of obduracy, and might be less sensible to the apprehension of suspicion or censure for an injudicious or affected clemency. On these accounts, one man appears to be a more eligible dispenser of the mercy of the government than a body of men. (No. 74)

IN SEASONS of insurrection or rebellion there are often critical moments when a well-timed offer of pardon to the insurgents or rebels may restore the tranquility of the commonwealth, and which if suffered to pass unimproved, it may never be possible afterwards to recall. The dilatory process of convening the Legislature or one of its branches, for the purpose of obtaining its sanction to the measure would frequently be the occasion of letting slip the golden opportunity. The loss of a week, a day, an hour, may sometimes be fatal. (No. 74)

[O]NE MAN OF discernment is better fitted to analyze and estimate the peculiar qualities adapted to particular offices than a body of men of equal, or perhaps even of superior discernment.

The sole and undivided responsibility of one man will naturally beget a livelier sense of duty and a more exact regard to reputation. He will, on this account, feel himself under stronger obligations, and more interested to investigate with care the qualities requisite to the stations to be filled, and to prefer with impartiality the persons who may have the fairest pretensions to them. He will have *fewer* personal attachments to gratify than a body of men who may each be supposed to have an equal number, and will be so much the less liable to be misled by the sentiments of friendship and of affection. A single well-directed man, by a single understanding, cannot be distracted and warped by that diversity of views, feelings, and interests which frequently distract and warp the resolutions of a collective body. There is nothing so apt to agitate the passions of mankind as personal considerations, whether they relate to ourselves, or to others who are to be the objects of our choice or preference. (No. 76)

To WHAT PURPOSE then require the cooperation of the Senate [in the matter of appointments]? I answer that the necessity of their concurrence would have a powerful, though in general, a silent operation. It would be an excellent check upon a spirit of favoritism in the President, and would tend greatly to preventing the appointment of unfit characters from State prejudice, from family connection, from personal attachment, or from a view to popularity. And in addition to this, it would be an efficacious source of stability in the administration.

It will readily be comprehended that a man who had himself the sole disposition of offices would be governed much more by his private inclinations and interests, than when he was bound to submit the propriety of his choice to the discussion and determination of a different and independent body; and that body an entire branch of the Legislature. The possibility of rejection would be a strong motive to care in proposing. The danger to his own reputation, and in the case of an elective magistrate, to his political existence, from betraying a spirit of favoritism or an unbecoming pursuit of popularity to the observation of a body whose opinion would have great weight in forming that of the public, could not fail to operate as a barrier to the one and to the other. He would be both ashamed and afraid to bring forward, for the most distinguished or lucrative stations, candidates who had no other merit than that of coming from the same State to which he particularly belonged, or of being in some way or other personally allied to him, or of possessing the necessary insignificance and pliancy to render them the obsequious instruments of his pleasure. (No. 76)

IT HAS BEEN mentioned as one of the advantages to be expected from the cooperation of the Senate in the business of appointments, that it would contribute to the stability of the administration. The consent of that body would be necessary to displace as well as to appoint.* A change of

---

*The issue of whether or not the consent of the Senate was required in order for the president to "discharge" or remove executive appointees was debated by the first Congress. In the course of establishing what became the State Department,

the chief magistrate, therefore, would not occasion so violent or so general a revolution in the officers of the government as might be expected if he were the sole disposer of offices. Where a man in any station had given satisfactory evidence of his fitness for it, a new president would be restrained from attempting a change in favor of a person more agreeable to him, by the apprehension that the discountenance of the Senate might frustrate the attempt, and bring some degree of discredit upon himself. Those who can best estimate the value of a steady administration will be most disposed to prize a provision which connects the official existence of public men with the approbation or disapprobation of that body, which from the greater permanency of its own composition, will in all probability be less subject to inconstancy than any other member of the government. (No. 77)

---

James Madison, who believed the Constitution vested the power of removal solely with the executive, proposed that the secretary for foreign affairs be "removable by the President" alone. The measure was carried in the House of Representatives, and passed in the Senate, but only after Vice-President John Adams cast the tie-breaking vote. Had Congress made the power of removal dependent upon the "advice and consent" of the Senate, the authority and independence of the executive branch would have been severely diminished. (Editor)

# 7

## Law and the Judiciary

Early in its deliberations, the Federal Convention agreed to establish a national judiciary composed of "one supreme tribunal" and "one or more inferior tribunals." It was also agreed that federal judges would be selected by the Senate and have life tenure during "good behavior." Later in the proceedings the delegates decided to leave the creation of "inferior" federal courts to the discretion of Congress and vested the appointment power with the president, subject to the approval of the upper house.

More vexing were attempts to (1) fix the jurisdiction of the federal courts, particularly in relation to existing state tribunals, and (2) ensure the independence of the judiciary. The former endeavor involved prickly issues of federalism, while the latter raised concerns over the separation of powers. Neither issue was completely settled by the Convention, which left important details regarding the judiciary's structure and jurisdiction to the determination of Congress.

The Framers did, however, determine that the federal judicial power would "extend to all Cases, in Law and Equity" arising under the Constitution, and to "the Laws of the United States and Treaties made . . . under their Authority." Federal jurisdiction would also extend to disputes involving the national government, as well controversies between a state and a citizen of another state, between citizens from different states, and between the states themselves. The Supreme Court was given original jurisdiction over disputes among the states, and in "all Cases affecting Ambassadors, other public Ministers and Consuls."

The Court's appellate jurisdiction, "in Law and in Fact," was made co-extensive with the federal judicial power, although subject to "exceptions" and "regulations" imposed by Congress. In addition to these Article III provisions, Article VI declared the Constitution, as well as treaties and federal statutes pursuant to the Constitution, the "supreme Law of the Land."

The Framers did not, however, (1) specify the method of appealing a state court decision to a federal tribunal, (2) fix the appellate jurisdiction of the Supreme Court (or even the number of justices), (3) determine the concurrent jurisdiction of state courts in federal and constitutional cases, or (4) grant the federal judiciary explicit power to nullify state laws which were in conflict with the Constitution, treaties, or laws of the United States. These and other provisions were established by the Judiciary Act passed by the first Congress in 1789.

Opponents of ratification viewed the proposed judiciary with grave suspicion. The Constitution's failure to guarantee jury trials in civil cases, trials of vicinage in criminal cases, as well as its broad grant of judicial power were frequently denounced as threats to individual liberty and the independence of the states. Such fears were addressed by Publius (Hamilton), who underscored the limits of federal jurisdiction and assured his readers that the judiciary "will always be the least dangerous" branch of the general government. Conversely, he argued that responsibility for upholding the supremacy and uniformity of federal law could not be entrusted to the state courts. Warning that the operation of thirteen separate judiciaries would produce "a hydra in government," Hamilton insisted that only a duly constituted national judiciary could vindicate the supreme law of the land. In addition to defending the Constitution's prohibition on lowering the salaries of federal judges, he characterized its provision for life tenure as "an indispensable ingredient" of judicial independence.

While the Judiciary Act of 1789 authorized the federal courts to strike down state laws deemed "repugnant" to federal law or the Constitution, it did not extend this power to acts of Congress. Indeed, the issue of "judicial review" was not raised directly in the Convention, nor did it figure prominently in the ratification debates. Yet in Federalist No. 78 Hamilton asserted that it was the "duty" of the judiciary to "declare all acts contrary to the manifest tenor of the Constitution void," including those passed by Congress. This power, he argued, was "deducible" from the very concept of a limited constitution and would be essential to its maintenance.

To the charge that the right to void acts of Congress elevated the judiciary to a position of supremacy, Hamilton responded that the "power of the people" (as embodied in the Constitution) was "superior to both." He also argued that both Congress and the executive were fully capable of withstanding encroachments by the judiciary, which possessed "neither Force nor Will, but merely judgment."

*The implications of Hamilton's endorsement of judicial review were not clarified until 1803 when the Supreme Court struck down a provision of the Judiciary Act of 1789. In asserting the right of the judicial branch "to say what the law is," Chief Justice John Marshall drew heavily upon the arguments of Publius. As a result,* Federalist No. 78 *became (and has remained) the* locus classicus *for the distinctively American doctrine of judicial review.*

GOVERNMENT implies the power of making laws. It is essential to the idea of a law that it be attended with a sanction, or in other words, a penalty or punishment for disobedience. If there be no penalty annexed to disobedience, the resolutions or commands which pretend to be laws will in fact amount to nothing more than advice or recommendation. (No. 15)

LAWS ARE a dead letter without courts to expound and define their true meaning and operation. (No. 22)

To AVOID the confusion which would unavoidably result from the contradictory decisions of a number of independent judicatories, all nations have found it necessary to establish one court paramount to the rest—possessing a general superintendence, and authorized to settle and declare in the last resort, a uniform rule of civil justice. (No. 22)

THE PROPRIETY of a law in a constitutional light must always be determined by the nature of the powers upon which it is founded. (No. 33)

THE STANDARD of good behavior for the continuance in office of the judicial magistracy is certainly one of the most valuable of the modern improvements in the practice of government. In a monarchy it is an excellent barrier to the despotism of the prince. In a republic it is a no less excellent barrier to the encroachments and oppressions of the representative body. And it is the best expedient which can be devised in any government to secure a steady, upright, and impartial administration of the laws. Whoever attentively considers the different departments of power must perceive that in a government in which they are separated from each other, the judiciary, from the nature of its functions, will always be the least dangerous to the political rights of the Constitution, because it will be least in a capacity to annoy or injure them. The executive not only dispenses the honors, but holds the sword of the community. The legislative not only commands the purse, but prescribes the rules by which the duties and rights of every citizen are to be regulated. The judiciary, on the contrary, has no influence over either the sword or the purse, no direction either of the strength or of the wealth of the society, and can take no active resolution whatever. It may truly be said to have neither FORCE nor WILL, but merely judgment, and must ultimately depend upon the aid of the executive arm even for the efficacy of its judgments.

This simple view of the matter suggests several important consequences. It proves incontestably that the judiciary is beyond comparison the weakest of the three departments of power;* that it can never attack with success either of the other two; and that all possible care is requisite to enable it to defend itself against their attacks. It equally proves that though individual oppression may now and then proceed from the courts of justice, the general liberty of the people can never be endangered from that quarter; I mean, so long as the judiciary remains truly distinct from both the legislative and executive. For I agree that "there is no liberty if the power of judging be not separated from the legislative and executive powers."† And it proves, in the last place, that as liberty can have nothing to fear from its judiciary alone, but would have everything to fear from its union with either of the other departments; that as all the effects of such a union must ensue from a dependence of the former on the latter, notwithstanding a nominal and apparent separation; that as from the natural feebleness of the judiciary, it is in continual jeopardy of being overpowered, awed, or influenced by its coordinate branches; and that as nothing can contribute so much to its firmness and independence as permanency in office, this quality may therefore be justly regarded as an indispensable ingredient in its constitution, and in a great measure as the citadel of the public justice and the public security.

The complete independence of the courts of justice is peculiarly essential in a limited constitution. By a limited constitution I understand one which contains certain specified exceptions to the legislative authority; such for instance, as that it shall pass no bills of attainder, no *ex post facto* laws, and the like. Limitations of this kind can be preserved in practice no other way than through the medium of the courts of justice, whose duty it must be to declare all acts contrary to the manifest tenor of the constitution void. Without this, all the reservations of particular rights or privileges would amount to nothing.

---

*The celebrated Montesquieu speaking of them says, "of the three powers above mentioned, the JUDICIARY is next to nothing." Spirit of Laws, vol. 1, page 186. (Publius)
    †Idem. page 181. (Publius)

Some perplexity respecting the right of the courts to pronounce legislative acts void, because contrary to the constitution, has arisen from an imagination that the doctrine would imply a superiority of the judiciary to the legislative power. It is urged that the authority which can declare the acts of another void must necessarily be superior to the one whose acts may be declared void. As this doctrine is of great importance in all the American constitutions, a brief discussion of the grounds on which it rests cannot be unacceptable.

There is no position which depends on clearer principles than that every act of a delegated authority contrary to the tenor of the commission under which it is exercised is void. No legislative act, therefore, contrary to the Constitution can be valid. To deny this would be to affirm that the deputy is greater than his principal; that the servant is above his master; that the representatives of the people are superior to the people themselves; that men acting by virtue of powers may do not only what their powers do not authorize, but what they forbid.

If it be said that the legislative body are themselves the constitutional judges of their own powers, and that the construction they put upon them is conclusive upon the other departments, it may be answered that this cannot be the natural presumption where it is not to be collected from any particular provisions in the Constitution. It is not otherwise to be supposed that the Constitution could intend to enable the representatives of the people to substitute their *will* to that of their constituents. It is far more rational to suppose that the courts were designed to be an intermediate body between the people and the legislature in order, among other things, to keep the latter within the limits assigned to their authority. The interpretation of the laws is the proper and peculiar province of the courts. A constitution is in fact, and must be, regarded by the judges as a fundamental law. It therefore belongs to them to ascertain its meaning, as well as the meaning of any particular act proceeding from the legislative body. If there should happen to be an irreconcilable variance between the two, that which has the superior obligation and validity ought, of course, to be preferred; or in other words, the Constitution ought to be preferred to the statute, the intention of the people to the intention of their agents.

Nor does this conclusion by any means suppose a superiority of the judicial to the legislative power. It only supposes that the power of the people is superior to both; and that where the will of the legislature declared in its statutes stands in opposition to that of the people declared in the Constitution, the judges ought to be governed by the latter, rather than the former. They ought to regulate their decisions by the fundamental laws, rather than by those which are not fundamental.

This exercise of judicial discretion in determining between two contradictory laws is exemplified in a familiar instance. It not uncommonly happens that there are two statutes existing at one time, clashing in whole or in part with each other, and neither of them containing any repealing clause or expression. In such a case, it is the province of the courts to liquidate and fix their meaning and operation. So far as they can by any fair construction be reconciled to each other, reason and law conspire to dictate that this should be done. Where this is impracticable, it becomes a matter of necessity to give effect to one, in exclusion of the other. The rule which has obtained in the courts for determining their relative validity is that the last in order of time shall be preferred to the first. But this is mere rule of construction, not derived from any positive law, but from the nature and reason of the thing. It is a rule not enjoined upon the courts by legislative provision, but adopted by themselves, as consonant to truth and propriety, for the direction of their conduct as interpreters of the law. They thought it reasonable that between the interfering acts of an *equal* authority, that which was the last indication of its will should have the preference.

But in regard to the interfering acts of a superior and subordinate authority of an original and derivative power, the nature and reason of the thing indicate the converse of that rule as proper to be followed. They teach us that the prior act of a superior ought to be preferred to the subsequent act of an inferior and subordinate authority; and that, accordingly, whenever a particular statute contravenes the Constitution, it will be the duty of the judicial tribunals to adhere to the latter and disregard the former.

It can be of no weight to say that the courts, on the pretense of a repugnancy, may substitute their own pleasure to the constitutional intentions of the legislature. This might as well happen in the case of two contradictory statutes, or it might as well happen in every adjudication upon any single statute. The courts must declare the sense of the law; and if they should be disposed to exercise Will instead of Judgment, the consequence would equally be the substitution of their pleasure to that of the legislative body. The observation, if it proved anything, would prove that there ought to be no judges distinct from that body.

If then the courts of justice are to be considered as the bulwarks of a limited constitution against legislative encroachments, this consideration will afford a strong argument for the permanent tenure of judicial offices, since nothing will contribute so much as this to that independent spirit in the judges, which must be essential to the faithful performance of so arduous a duty.

This independence of the judges is equally requisite to guard the Constitution and the rights of individuals from the effects of those ill humors which the arts of designing men, or the influence of particular conjunctures, sometimes disseminate among the people themselves, and which, though they speedily give place to better information and more deliberate reflection, have a tendency in the mean time to occasion dangerous innovations in the government, and serious oppressions of the minor party in the community. Though I trust the friends of the proposed Constitution will never concur with its enemies in questioning that fundamental principle of republican government, which admits the right of the people to alter or abolish the established constitution whenever they find it inconsistent with their happiness. Yet it is not to be inferred from this principle that the representatives of the people, whenever a momentary inclination happens to lay hold of a majority of their constituents incompatible with the provisions in the existing constitution, would on that account be justifiable in a violation of those provisions; or that the courts would be under a greater obligation to connive at infractions in this shape, than when they had proceeded wholly from the cabals of the representative body. Until the people have by some solemn and authoritative act annulled or changed the established form, it is binding upon themselves collectively, as well as individually; and no presumption, or even knowledge of their sentiments can warrant their representatives in a departure from it prior to such an act. But it is easy to see that it would require an uncommon portion of fortitude in the judges to do their duty as faithful guardians of the Constitution, where legislative invasions of it had been instigated by the major voice of the community.

But it is not with a view to infractions of the Constitution only that the independence of the judges may be an essential safeguard against the effects of occasional ill humors in the society. These sometimes extend no farther than to the injury of the private rights of particular classes of citizens by unjust and partial laws. Here also the firmness of the judicial magistracy is of vast importance in mitigating the severity, and confining the operation of such laws. It not only serves to moderate the immediate mischiefs of those which may have been passed, but it operates as a check upon the legislative body in passing them; who, perceiving that obstacles to the success of an iniquitous intention are to be expected from the scruples of the courts, are in a manner compelled by the very motives of the injustice they meditate to qualify their attempts. This is a circumstance calculated to have more influence upon the character of our governments than but few may be aware of. The benefits of the integrity and moderation of the judiciary have already been felt in more states than one; and though they may have displeased those whose sinister expectations they may have disappointed, they must have commanded the esteem and applause of all the virtuous and disinterested. Considerate men of every description ought to prize whatever will tend to beget or fortify that temper in the courts; as no man can be sure that he may not be tomorrow the victim of a spirit of injustice by which he may be a gainer today. And every man must now feel that the inevitable tendency of such a spirit is to sap the foundations of public and private confidence, and to introduce in its stead, universal distrust and distress.

That inflexible and uniform adherence to the rights of the Constitution and of individuals which we perceive to be indispensable in the courts of justice, can certainly not be expected from judges who hold their offices by a temporary commission. Periodical appointments, however regulated or by whomsoever made, would in some way or other be fatal to their necessary independence. If the power of making them was committed either to the executive or legislative, there would be danger of an improper complaisance to the branch which possessed it; if to both, there would be an unwillingness to hazard the displeasure of either; if to the people, or to persons chosen by them for the special purpose, there would be too great a disposition to consult popularity, to justify a reliance that nothing would be consulted but the Constitution and the laws.

There is yet a further and a weighty reason for the permanency of the judicial offices, which is deducible from the nature of the qualifications they require. It has been frequently remarked with great propriety, that a voluminous code of laws is one of the inconveniences necessarily connected with the advantages of a free government. To avoid an arbitrary discretion in the courts, it is indispensable that they should be bound down by strict rules and precedents which serve to define and point out their duty in every particular case that comes before them; and it will readily be conceived from the variety of controversies which grow out of the folly and wickedness of mankind, that the records of those precedents must unavoidably swell to a very considerable bulk, and must demand long and laborious study to acquire a competent knowledge of them. Hence it is that there can be but few men in the society who will have sufficient skill in the laws to qualify them for the stations of judges. And making the proper deductions for the ordinary depravity of human nature, the number must be still smaller of those who unite the requisite integrity with the requisite knowledge. These considerations apprise us that the government can have no great option between fit characters; and that a temporary duration in office, which would naturally discourage such characters from quitting a lucrative line of practice to accept a seat on the bench, would have a tendency to throw the administration of justice into hands less able and less well qualified to conduct it with utility and dignity. In the present circumstances of this country, and in those in which it is likely to be for a long time to come, the disadvantages on this score would be greater than they may at first sight appear; but it must be confessed that they are far inferior to those which present themselves under the other aspects of the subject.

Upon the whole there can be no room to doubt that the Convention acted wisely in copying from the models of those constitutions which have established *good behavior* as the tenure of their judicial offices in point of duration; and that so far from being blameable on this account, their plan would have been inexcusably defective if it had wanted this important feature of good government. The experience of Great Britain affords an illustrious comment on the excellence of the institution. (No. 78)

THE SALARIES of judicial offices may from time to time be altered as occasion shall require, yet so as never to lessen the allowance with which any particular judge comes into office in respect to him. It will be observed that a difference has been made by the Convention between the compensation of the president and of the judges. That of the former can neither be increased nor diminished. That of the latter can only not be diminished. This probably arose from the difference in the duration of the respective offices. As the president is to be elected for no more than four years, it can rarely happen that an adequate salary, fixed at the commencement of that period, will not continue to be such to the end of it. But with regard to the judges who, if they behave properly, will be secured in their places for life, it may well happen, especially in the early stages of the government, that a stipend, which would be very sufficient at their first appointment, would become too small in the progress of their service.

This provision for the support of the judges bears every mark of prudence and efficacy; and it may be safely affirmed that, together with the permanent tenure of their offices, it affords a better prospect of their independence than is discoverable in the constitutions of any of the states in regard to their own judges. (No. 79)

THE WANT of a provision for removing the judges on account of inability has been a subject of complaint. But all considerate men will be sensible that such a provision would either not be practiced upon, or would be more liable to abuse than calculated to answer any good purpose. The mensuration of the faculties of the mind has, I believe, no place in the catalogue of known arts. An attempt to fix the boundary between the regions of ability and inability would much oftener give scope to personal and party attachments and enmities, than advance the interests of justice, or the public good. The result, except in the case of insanity, must for the most part be arbitrary; and insanity without any formal or express provision may be safely pronounced to be a virtual disqualification. (No. 79)

THE DELIBERATING and comparing faculties generally preserve their strength much beyond [the age of sixty] in men who survive it; and when in addition to this circumstance, we consider how few there are who outlive the season of intellectual vigor, and how improbable it is that any considerable proportion of the bench, whether more or less numerous, should be in such a situation at the same time, we shall be ready to conclude that limitations of this sort have little to recommend them. In a republic, where fortunes are not affluent and pensions not expedient, the dismissal of men from stations in which they have served their country long and usefully, on which they depend for subsistence, and from which it will be too late to resort to any other occupation for a livelihood, ought to have some better apology to humanity than is to be found in the imaginary danger of a superannuated bench. (No. 79)

No MAN of sense will believe that . . . prohibitions [on the states] would be scrupulously regarded without some effectual power in the government to restrain or correct the infractions of them. This power must either be a direct negative on the state laws, or an authority in the federal courts to overrule such as might be in manifest contravention of the articles of union. There is no third course that I can imagine. The latter appears to have been thought by the Convention preferable to the former, and I presume will be most agreeable to the states. (No. 80)

IF THERE are such things as political axioms, the propriety of the judicial power of a government being coextensive with its legislative may be ranked among the number. The mere necessity of uniformity in the interpretation of the national laws decides the question. Thirteen independent courts of final jurisdiction over the same causes, arising upon the same laws, is a hydra in government from which nothing but contradiction and confusion can proceed. (No. 80)

CONTROVERSIES BETWEEN the nation and its members or citizens can only be properly referred to the national tribunals. Any other plan would be contrary to reason, to precedent, and to decorum. (No. 80)

[I]N ORDER TO the inviolable maintenance of that equality of privileges and immunities to which the citizens of the union will be entitled, the national judiciary ought to preside in all cases in which one state or its citizens are opposed to another state or its citizens. To secure the full effect of so fundamental a provision against all evasion and subterfuge, it is necessary that its construction should be committed to that tribunal, which, having no local attachments, will be likely to be impartial between the different states and their citizens and which owing its official existence to the union will never be likely to feel any bias inauspicious to the principles on which it is founded. (No. 80)

THE MOST bigoted idolizers of state authority have not thus far shown a disposition to deny the national judiciary the cognizance of maritime causes. These so generally depend on the laws of nations, and so commonly affect the rights of foreigners, that they fall within the considerations which are relative to the public peace (No. 80).

THE REASONABLENESS of the agency of the national courts in cases in which the state tribunals cannot be supposed to be impartial speaks for itself. No man ought certainly to be a judge in his own cause, or in any cause in respect to which he has the least interest or bias. This principle has no inconsiderable weight in designating the federal courts as the proper tribunals for the determination of controversies between different states and their citizens. And it ought to have the same operation in regard to some cases between the citizens of the same state. (No. 80)

[T]HOUGH [a supreme court composed of senators] be not an absolute violation of that excellent rule [separation of powers]; yet it verges so nearly upon it, as on this account alone to be less eligible than the mode preferred by the Convention. From a body which had had even a partial agency in passing bad laws, we could rarely expect a disposition to temper and moderate them in the application. The same spirit which had operated in making them would be too apt to operate in interpreting them. Still less could it be expected that men who had infringed the Constitution, in the character of legislators would be disposed to repair the breach in the character of judges. Nor is this all: Every reason which recommends the tenure of good behavior for judicial offices, militates against placing the judiciary power, in the last resort, in a body composed of men chosen for a limited period. There is an absurdity in referring the determination of causes in the first instance to judges of permanent standing, and in the last to those of a temporary and mutable constitution. And there is a still greater absurdity in subjecting the decisions of men selected for their knowledge of the laws, acquired by long and laborious study, to the revision and control of men, who for want of the same advantage, cannot but be deficient in that knowledge. The members of the legislature will rarely be chosen with a view to those qualifications which fit men for the stations of judges; and as on this account there will be great reason to apprehend all the ill consequences of defective information. So on account of the natural propensity of such bodies to party divisions, there will be no less reason to fear that the pestilential breath of faction may poison the fountains of justice. The habit of being continually marshaled on opposite sides will be too apt to stifle the voice both of law and of equity.

These considerations teach us to applaud the wisdom of those states who have committed the judicial power in the last resort, not to a part of the legislature, but to distinct and independent bodies of men. (No. 81)

THE POWER of constituting inferior courts is evidently calculated to obviate the necessity of having recourse to the Supreme Court in every case of federal cognizance. It is intended to enable the national government to institute or *authorize* in each state or district of the United States, a tribunal competent to the determination of matters of national jurisdiction within its limits. (No. 81)

THE MOST discerning cannot foresee how far the prevalence of a local spirit may be found to disqualify the local tribunals for the jurisdiction of national causes; whilst every man may discover that courts constituted like those of some of the states would be improper channels of the judicial authority of the union. State judges, holding their offices during pleasure or from year to year, will be too little independent to be relied upon for an inflexible execution of the national laws. (No. 81)

To AVOID all inconveniences, it will be safest to declare generally that the Supreme Court shall possess appellate jurisdiction, both as to law and *fact*, and that this jurisdiction shall be subject to such *exceptions* and regulations as the national legislature may prescribe. This will enable the government to modify it in such a manner as will best answer the ends of public justice and security. (No. 81)

[T]HE AUTHORITY of the judicial department . . . has been carefully restricted to those causes which are manifestly proper for the cognizance of the national judicature; that in the partition of this authority a very small portion of original jurisdiction has been reserved to the Supreme

Court, and the rest consigned to the subordinate tribunals; that the Supreme Court will possess an appellate jurisdiction both as to law and fact in all the cases referred to them, but subject to any *exceptions* and *regulations* which may be thought advisable. (No. 81)

THE JUDICIARY POWER of every government looks beyond its own local or municipal laws, and in civil cases lays hold of all subjects of litigation between parties within its jurisdiction, though the causes of dispute are relative to the laws of the most distant part of the globe. Those of Japan not less than of New York may furnish the objects of legal discussion to our courts. When in addition to this, we consider the state governments and the national government as they truly are, in the light of kindred systems and as parts of ONE WHOLE, the inference seems to be conclusive that the state courts would have a concurrent jurisdiction in all cases arising under the laws of the union where it was not expressly prohibited. (No. 82)

THE CONSTITUTION, in direct terms, gives an appellate jurisdiction to the Supreme Court in all the enumerated cases of federal cognizance in which it is not to have an original one, without a single expression to confine its operation to the inferior federal courts. The objects of appeal, not the tribunals from which it is to be made, are alone contemplated. From this circumstance and from the reason of the thing, it ought to be construed to extend to the state tribunals. Either this must be the case, or the local [state] courts must be excluded from a concurrent jurisdiction in matters of national concern, else the judicial authority of the union may be eluded at the pleasure of every plaintiff or prosecutor. Neither of these consequences ought without evident necessity to be involved; the latter would be entirely inadmissible, as it would defeat some of the most important and avowed purposes of the proposed government, and would essentially embarrass its measures. Nor do I perceive any foundation for such a supposition. Agreeably to the remark already made, the national and state systems are to be regarded as ONE WHOLE. The courts of the latter will of course be natural auxiliaries to the execution of the laws of the Union, and an appeal from them will as naturally lie to that tribunal which is destined to unite and assimilate the principles of national justice and the rules of national decisions. The evident aim of the plan of the Convention is that all the causes of the specified classes shall for weighty public reasons receive their original or final determination in the courts of the union. To confine therefore the general expressions giving appellate jurisdiction to the Supreme Court to appeals from the subordinate federal courts, instead of allowing their extension to the state courts, would be to abridge the latitude of the terms in subversion of the intent, contrary to every sound rule of interpretation. (No. 82)

I PERCEIVE AT present no impediment to the establishment of an appeal from the state courts to the subordinate national tribunals; and many advantages attending the power of doing it may be imagined. It would diminish the motives to the multiplication of federal courts, and would admit of arrangements calculated to contract the appellate jurisdiction of the Supreme Court. The state tribunals may then be left with a more entire charge of federal causes; and appeals in most cases in which they may be deemed proper, instead of being carried to the Supreme Court, may be made to lie from the state courts to district courts of the union. (No. 82)

THE RULES OF legal interpretation are rules of *common sense*, adopted by the courts in the construction of the laws. The true test, therefore, of a just application of them is its conformity to the source from which they are derived. (No. 83)

THE PLAN OF the Convention declares that the power of Congress, or in other words, of the *national legislature*, shall extend to certain enumerated cases. This specification of particulars evidently excludes all pretension to a general legislative authority; because an affirmative grant of special powers would be absurd as well as useless if a general authority was intended.

In like manner, the judicial authority of the federal judiciary is declared by the Constitution to comprehend certain cases particularly specified. The expression of those cases marks the precise limits beyond which the federal courts cannot extend their jurisdiction; because the objects of their cognizance being enumerated, the specification would be nugatory if it did not exclude all ideas of more extensive authority. (No. 83)

# 8

Political Economy

Among the gravest defects of the Articles of Confederation was its failure to vest Congress with the means of raising a revenue sufficient to the basic needs of the national government. More than once America's struggle for independence nearly foundered on the rock of insolvency, as witnessed by the hardships endured by the ill-supplied Continental Army. Following the victory at Yorktown in October 1781 the government's financial difficulties only worsened. Frustrated with the ineptitude of Congress, a cabal of army officers and politicians flirted with the idea of coup in March 1783. Later that year a group of unpaid soldiers mutinied, marched on Philadelphia, and drove Congress from its seat. Yet the nation's fiscal plight owed less to the failure of Congress than to the Articles themselves, which denied that body the power to levy and collect taxes. Congress was authorized to make "requisitions" from the states, but could not enforce compliance, and contributions to the general coffers were irregular at best. On two occasions a revenue amendment was approved by twelve of the thirteen states, but the requirement of unanimous consent in such cases prevented its adoption.

The depth of the crisis was apparent to Madison and Hamilton even before the Articles were officially ratified in March 1781. As members of Congress both men proposed measures aimed at stabilizing the government's finances and procuring adequate sources of income. The failure of their efforts persuaded them *(and many others) that a more fundamental reform was required if the Union was to survive and prosper. Under the Articles, Congress had neither the power to tax nor the authority to regulate commerce or impose tariff duties. (Neither could it require states to honor legal contracts nor prohibit them from issuing their own currency.) As a result, the national government was chronically short of money and helpless to prevent the states from engaging in discriminatory economic policies. Such conditions (and the impossibility of alleviating them under the Articles) were instrumental in bringing about the Federal Convention of 1787.*

*The proposed Constitution gave the national government the fiscal, monetary, and commercial authority it had previously lacked. It was among the principal tasks of Publius to defend these grants of power—particularly the power to levy direct taxes—and to convince Americans that such measures were not merely desirable, but absolutely vital to the safety, unity, and prosperity of the nation. This task fell primarily to Hamilton, who possessed a remarkable grasp of the principles of political economy. While emphasizing the political necessity of procuring adequate sources of revenue for the government, Hamilton also stressed the economic benefits destined to result from a "common market" among the states. More contentious was his defense of the "unqualified power of taxation," which he called "the most important of the authorities . . . conferred upon the Union." As the future "exigencies" of the nation were not subject to limitation, Hamilton argued, it would be highly imprudent to limit the central government's capacity to meet its financial needs. Moreover, he stressed the need for expertise, restraint, and a "knowledge of local circumstances" in constructing a non-oppressive tax code that would encourage economic growth.*

*Hamilton suggested that responsibility for fiscal policy should reside with the executive branch and recommended measures central to the economic program he would champion as secretary of the treasury. Moreover, he articulated a compelling vision of America's economic destiny under the Constitution; a vision he would help forge into a reality in the Washington administration.*

FOR IT IS an observation as true as it is trite, that there is nothing men differ so readily about as the payment of money. (No. 7)

THE IMPORTANCE OF the Union in a commercial light is one of those points about which there is least room to entertain a difference of opinion, and which has in fact commanded the most general assent of men who have any acquaintance with the subject. This applies as well to our intercourse with foreign countries as with each other.

There are appearances to authorize a supposition that the adventurous spirit which distinguishes the commercial character of America, has already excited uneasy sensations in several of the maritime powers of Europe. They seem to be apprehensive of our too great interference in that carrying trade which is the support of their navigation and the foundation of their naval strength. Those of them which have colonies in America look forward to what this country is capable of becoming with painful solicitude. They foresee the dangers that may threaten their American dominions from the neighborhood of States which have all the dispositions, and would possess all the means requisite to the creation of a powerful marine. Impressions of this kind will naturally indicate the policy of fostering divisions among us, and of depriving us as far as possible of an ACTIVE COMMERCE in our own bottoms. This would answer the threefold purpose of preventing our interference in their navigation, of monopolizing the profits of our trade, and of clipping the wings by which we might soar to a dangerous greatness. Did not prudence forbid the detail, it would not be difficult to trace by facts the workings of this policy to the cabinets of [European] Ministers.

If we continue united we may counteract a policy so unfriendly to our prosperity in a variety of ways. By prohibitory regulations, extending at the same time throughout the States, we may oblige foreign countries to bid against each other for the privileges of our markets. This assertion will not appear chimerical to those who are able to appreciate the importance of the markets of three millions of people—increasing in rapid progression, for the most part exclusively addicted to agriculture, and likely from local circumstances to remain so—to any manufacturing nation; and the immense difference there would be to the trade and navigation of such a nation, between a direct communication in its own ships, and an indirect conveyance of its products and returns to and from America in the ships of another country. (No. 11)

AN UNRESTRAINED intercourse between the States themselves will advance the trade of each by an interchange of their respective productions, not only for the supply of reciprocal wants at home, but for exportation to foreign markets. The veins of commerce in every part will be replenished, and will acquire additional motion and vigor from a free circulation of the commodities of every part. Commercial enterprise will have much greater scope from the diversity in the productions of different States. When the staple of one fails from a bad harvest or unproductive crop, it can call to its aid the staple of another. The variety, not less than the value of products for exportation, contributes to the activity of foreign commerce. (No. 11)

A UNITY OF commercial as well as political interests can only result from a unity of government. (No. 11)

THE PROSPERITY of commerce is now perceived and acknowledged by all enlightened statesmen to be the most useful as well as the most productive source of national wealth, and has accordingly become a primary object of their political cares. By multiplying the means of gratification, by promoting the introduction and circulation of the precious metals and those darling objects of human avarice and enterprise, it serves to vivify and invigorate the channels of industry, and to make them flow with greater activity and copiousness. The assiduous merchant, the laborious husbandmen, the active mechanic, and the industrious manufacturer; all orders of men look forward with eager expectation and growing alacrity to this pleasing reward of their toils. (No. 12)

IT IS astonishing that so simple a truth [that an expanded commerce enhances the value of land] should ever have had an adversary; and it is one among a multitude of proofs, how apt a spirit of ill-informed jealousy, or of too great abstraction and refinement is to lead men astray from the plainest paths of reason and conviction. (No. 12)

THE ABILITY OF a country to pay taxes must always be proportioned in a great degree to the quantity of money in circulation, and to the celerity with which it circulates. Commerce, contributing to both these objects, must of necessity render the payment of taxes easier, and facilitate the requisite supplies to the treasury. (No. 12)

THE SINGLE article of ardent spirits, under Federal regulation, might be made to furnish a considerable revenue . . . [T]he whole quantity imported into the United States may be estimated at four millions of gallons: which at a shilling per gallon would produce two hundred thousand pounds. That article would well bear this rate of duty; and if it should tend to diminish the consumption of it, such an effect would be equally favorable to the agriculture, to the economy, to the morals and to the health of society. There is perhaps nothing so much a subject of national extravagance as these spirits. (No. 12)

THE WEALTH of nations depends upon an infinite variety of causes. Situation, soil, climate, the nature of the productions, the nature of the government, the genius of the citizens, the degree of information they possess, the state of commerce, of arts, of industry: these circumstances

and many much too complex, minute, or adventitious to admit of a particular specification, occasion differences hardly conceivable in the relative
opulence and riches of different countries. (No. 21)

IT IS A signal advantage of taxes on articles of consumption that they
contain in their own nature a security against excess. They prescribe
their own limit, which cannot be exceeded without defeating the end
proposed; that is, an extension of the revenue. (No. 21)

IN A branch of taxation [on land] where no limits to the discretion of the
government are to be found in the nature of things, the establishment of
a fixed rule, not incompatible with the end, may be attended with fewer
inconveniences than to leave that discretion altogether at large. (No. 21)

MONEY IS with propriety considered as the vital principle of the body politic,
as that which sustains its life and motion, and enables it to perform its most
essential functions. A complete power, therefore, to procure a regular and
adequate supply of it, as far as the resources of the community will permit,
may be regarded as an indispensable ingredient in every constitution. From
a deficiency in this particular, one of two evils must ensue: either the people
must be subjected to continual plunder as a substitute for a more eligible
mode of supplying the public wants, or the government must sink into a
fatal atrophy, and in a short course of time perish. (No. 30)

A GOVERNMENT ought to contain in itself every power requisite to the full
accomplishment of the objects committed to its care, and to the complete
execution of the trusts for which it is responsible; free from every other
control, but a regard to the public good and to the sense of the people.

As the duties superintending the national defense and of securing
the public peace against foreign or domestic violence involve a provision
for casualties and dangers to which no possible limits can be assigned,
the power of making that provision ought to know no other bounds than
the exigencies of the nation and the resources of the community.

As revenue is the essential engine by which the means of answering
the national exigencies must be procured, the power of procuring that
article in its full extent must necessarily be comprehended in that of providing for those exigencies.

As theory and practice conspire to prove that the power of procuring revenue is unavailing when exercised over the States in their collective
capacities, the Federal government must of necessity be invested with an
unqualified power of taxation in the ordinary modes. (No. 31)

[THE GENERAL taxing power] is the most important of the authorities proposed to be conferred upon the Union. (No. 33)

[I]t cannot be denied to be a just priciple, that in framing a constitution
of government for a nation, we ought, in those provisions which are
designed to be permanent, to calculate, not on temporary, but on permanent causes of expense. (No. 34)

THERE IS NO part of the administration of government that requires extensive information and a thorough knowledge of the principles of
political economy so much as the business of taxation. The man who
understands those principles best will be least likely to resort to oppressive expedients, or to sacrifice any particular class of citizens to the
procurement of revenue. It might be demonstrated that the most productive system of finance will always be the least burdensome. There can be
no doubt that in order to have a judicious exercise of the power of taxation it
is necessary that the person in whose hands it is should be acquainted with
the general genius, habits, and modes of thinking of the people at large, and
with the resources of the country. And this is all that can be reasonably
meant by a knowledge of the interests and feelings of the people. In any
other sense, the proposition has either no meaning or an absurd one. And in
that sense let every considerate citizen judge for himself where the requisite
qualification is most likely to be found. (No. 35)

NATIONS IN general, even under governments of the more popular kind,
usually commit the administration of their finances to single men or to
boards composed of a few individuals who digest and prepare, in the first
instance, the plans of taxation which are afterwards passed into laws by
the authority of the sovereign or Legislature.
       Inquisitive and enlightened Statesmen are deemed everywhere best
qualified to make a judicious selection of the objects proper for revenue; which is a clear indication, as far as the sense of mankind can
have weight in the question, of the species of knowledge of local circumstances requisite to the purposes of taxation. (No. 36)

IT IS now no longer a point of speculation and hope that the Western
territory is a mine of vast wealth to the United States. (No. 38)

As LONG as agriculture continues the sole field of labor, the importation
of manufactures must increase as the consumers multiply. As soon as
domestic manufactures are begun by the hands not called for by agricul-

ture, the imported manufactures will decrease as the numbers of people increase. In a more remote stage, the imports may consist in considerable part of raw materials which will be wrought into articles for exportation, and will therefore require rather the encouragement of bounties than to be loaded with discouraging duties. A system of Government meant for duration ought to contemplate these revolutions, and be able to accommodate itself to them. (No. 41)

HAD EVERY State a right to regulate the value of its coin, there might be as many different currencies as States; and thus the intercourse among them would be impeded. Retrospective alterations in its value might be made, and thus the citizens of other States be injured, and animosities be kindled among the States themselves. (No. 44)

# 9

——◆——

# Domestic Tranquility and the Common Defense

$T$ODAY IT IS DIFFICULT TO APPRECIATE *the precarious condition of the United States in the period following the Revolutionary War. In addition to the grave financial crisis, the new nation faced a number of internal and external threats to its welfare and security. Among the most troubling were (1) the failure of Great Britain to abandon its string of forts and trading posts along the Great Lakes as required by the Treaty of Paris (1783); (2) the decision of Spain to close the lower Mississippi River to American commerce; and (3) the inability of the national government to defend the western frontier against Indian raids. In addition to these difficulties, individual states openly violated the Paris treaty by enacting laws obstructing the collection of debts owed to British creditors and confiscating the property of Loyalists. The nation's financial troubles only exacerbated matters. Without money for an army or a navy, Congress could neither provide for domestic security, nor protect America's merchant marine from foreign attack. Such "imbecility" in government was dramatically confirmed when Congress found itself powerless to suppress the uprising in western Massachusetts known as Shays' Rebellion.*

*The humiliating weakness and dangerous vulnerability of the United States during the "critical period" loomed like an ominous cloud over the deliberations in Philadelphia. Most of the delegates agreed that only a stronger national government could "insure domestic Tranquility, [and] provide for the common defence." Accordingly, Congress was granted a general taxing authority, as well as broad powers over the armed forces, including the power to raise and maintain a standing army and declare war. The president was made commander-in-chief of the military and was authorized to call the state militias into active service. Both Congress and the president were given power to "suppress Insurrections and repel Invasions." Moreover, treaties of the United States were declared the "supreme Law of the Land," which made their provisions binding on the states. With regard to foreign relations and diplomacy, the Constitution gave the president authority to make treaties and appoint ambassadors with the "advice and consent" of the Senate. The president was also authorized to "receive Ambassadors," the standard means of formally recognizing a foreign government.*

*The authors of* The Federalist *were well-informed on matters of foreign policy, particularly John Jay, who was minister to Spain and a negotiator of the Treaty of Paris before becoming Secretary for Foreign Affairs in 1784. In urging the adoption of the Constitution, Publius emphasized the fatal dangers of military weakness, including a crippled commerce, civil war, disunion, and foreign conquest. Conversely, he highlighted the great advantages of military strength and preparedness. More specifically, Publius observed that American weakness would only encourage external aggression and domestic intrigue, and that nothing less than a "vigorous national government" was required to meet such threats. As "peace or war will not always be left to our option," he argued, it was essential that the United States maintain a respectable military force. As the Revolutionary War had shown, a citizen militia was no match for a professional, "standing" army, nor was overseas commerce secure without a formidable navy. It was therefore necessary for America to establish a "regular and disciplined army" and "endeavor as soon as possible to have a navy." Only then could the United States "hope to become the Arbiter of Europe in America," and thereby "dictate the terms of the connection between the Old and the New World." Such a force, and the authority to use it effectively, would also furnish the essential means for quelling domestic disturbances in a timely manner.*

*To those who argued that the Constitution did not place sufficient restrictions on this authority, Publius (Hamilton) was emphatic in expressing his "aversion to every project that is calculated to disarm the government of a single weapon which in any possible contingency might be usefully employed for the general defense and security." Just as the general government could not reasonably foresee its future financial needs, Hamilton asserted, neither could it precisely anticipate its future security needs.*

*In addition to the foregoing concerns, Publius also wrote in support of vesting the treaty-making power with the president and the Senate. Such an arrangement not only provided a check on this important power, but it promised to have "every advantage which can be derived from talents, information, and deliberative investigations on the one hand, and from secrecy and dispatch on the other." To have included the House of Representatives in the process, as some critics wanted, would have sacrificed "those qualities which are essential to the proper execution of such a trust." Here, as with the Constitution's other provisions for military and diplomatic powers, posterity appears to have vindicated the judgment of Publius.*

AMONG THE many objects to which a wise and free people find it necessary to direct their attention, that of providing for their *safety* seems to be the first. The *safety* of the people doubtless has relation to a great variety of circumstances and considerations, and consequently affords great latitude to those who wish to define it precisely and comprehensively. (No. 3)

IT IS TOO true, however disgraceful it may be to human nature, that nations in general will make war whenever they have a prospect of getting anything by it. (No. 4)

IT WAS remarked in the preceding Paper that weakness and divisions at home would invite dangers from abroad, and that nothing would tend more to secure us from them than Union, strength, and good Government within ourselves. (No. 5)

THE CAUSES of hostility among nations are innumerable. There are some which have a general and almost constant operation upon the collective bodies of society. Of this description are the love of power or the desire of preeminence and dominion—the jealousy of power, or the desire of equality and safety. There are others which have a more circumscribed, though an equally operative influence within their spheres: such are the rivalries and competitions of commerce between commercial nations. And there are others, not less numerous than either of the former, which take their origin entirely in private passions; in the attachments, enmities, interests, hopes and fears of leading individuals in the communities of which they are members. Men of this class, whether the favorites of a king or a people, have in too many instances abused the confidence they possessed; and assuming the pretext of some public motive, have not scrupled to sacrifice the national tranquility to personal advantage or personal gratification. (No. 6)

TERRITORIAL DISPUTES have at all times been found one of the most fertile sources of hostility among nations. Perhaps the greatest proportion of the wars that have desolated the earth have sprung from this origin. (No. 7)

PLUNDER AND devastation ever march in the train of irregulars. (No. 8)

SAFETY FROM external danger is the most powerful director of national conduct. Even the ardent love of liberty will, after a time, give way to its dictates. The violent destruction of life and property incident to war— the continual effort and alarm attendant on a state of continual danger, will compel nations the most attached to liberty to resort for repose and security to institutions which have a tendency to destroy their civil and political rights. To be more safe, they at length become willing to run the risk of being less free. (No. 8)

IF WE ARE wise enough to preserve the Union, we may for ages enjoy an advantage similar to that of an insulated situation. . . . But if we should be disunited, and the integral parts should either remain separated, or which is most probable, should be thrown together into two or three confederacies, we should be in a short course of time in the predicament of the continental powers of Europe—our liberties would be a prey to the means of defending ourselves against the ambition and jealousy of each other. (No. 8)

A FURTHER RESOURCE for influencing the conduct of European nations towards us . . . would arise from the establishment of a federal navy. There can be no doubt that the continuance of the Union under an efficient government would put it in our power, at a period not very distant, to create a navy, which, if it could not vie with those of the great maritime powers, would at least be of respectable weight if thrown into the scale of either of two contending parties. . . . A few ships of the line sent opportunely to the reinforcement of either side would often be sufficient to decide the fate of a campaign, on the event of which interests of the greatest magnitude were suspended. Our position is in this respect a very commanding one. . . . A price would be set not only upon our friendship, but upon our neutrality. By a steady adherence to the Union we may hope ere long to become the Arbiter of Europe in America, and to be able to incline the balance of European competitions in this part of the world as our interest may dictate.

But in the reverse of this eligible situation we shall discover that the rivalries of the parts would make them checks upon each other, and would frustrate all the tempting advantages which nature has kindly placed within our reach. In a state so insignificant, our commerce would be a prey to the wanton intermeddlings of all nations at war with each other, who having nothing to fear from us, would with little scruple or remorse supply their wants by depredations on our property, as often as it fell in their way. The rights of neutrality will only be respected when they are defended by an adequate power. A nation despicable by its weakness forfeits even the privilege of being neutral.

Under a vigorous national government, the natural strength and resources of the country directed to a common interest would baffle all the combinations of European jealousy to restrain our growth. This situation would even take away the motive to such combinations by inducing an impracticability of success. An active commerce, an extensive navigation, and a flourishing marine would then be the inevitable offspring of moral and physical necessity. We might defy the little arts of little politicians to control, or vary the irresistible and unchangeable course of nature.

But in a state of disunion these combinations might exist, and might operate with success. It would be in the power of the maritime nations, availing themselves of our universal impotence, to prescribe the conditions of our political existence; and as they have a common interest in being our carriers, and still more in preventing our being theirs, they would in all probability combine to embarrass our navigation in such a manner as would in effect destroy it, and confine us to a PASSIVE COMMERCE. We should thus be compelled to content ourselves with the first price of our commodities, and to see the profits of our trade snatched from us to enrich our enemies and persecutors. That unequalled spirit of enterprise which signals the genius of the American Merchants and Navigators, and which is in itself an inexhaustible mine of national wealth, would be stifled and lost; and poverty and disgrace would overspread a country, which with wisdom might make herself the admiration and envy of the world. (No. 11)

[O]UR SITUATION invites, and our interests prompt us to aim, at an ascendent in the system of American affairs. The world may politically, as well as geographically, be divided into four parts, each having a distinct set of interests. Unhappily for the other three, Europe, by her arms and by her negotiations, by force and by fraud, has in different degrees, extended her dominion over them all. Africa, Asia, and America have successively felt her domination. The superiority she has long maintained has tempted her to plume herself as the Mistress of the World, and to consider the rest of mankind as created for her benefit. Men admired as profound philosophers have, in direct terms, attributed to her inhabitants a physical superiority, and have gravely asserted that all animals, and with them the human species, degenerate in America—that even dogs cease to bark after having breathed a while in our atmosphere. Facts have too long supported these arrogant pretensions of the European. It belongs to us to vindicate the honor of the human race, and to teach that assuming brother moderation. Union will enable us to do it. Disunion will add another victim to his triumphs. Let Americans disdain to be the instruments of European greatness! Let the thirteen States, bound together in a strict and indissoluble union, concur in erecting one great American system, superior to the control of all trans-Atlantic force or influence, and able to dictate the terms of the connection between the Old and the New World! (No. 11)

WHEN THE sword is once drawn, the passions of men observe no bounds of moderation. (No. 16)

THE MAGISTRACY, being equally the Ministers of the law of the land, from whatever source it might emanate, would doubtless be as ready to guard the national as the local regulations from the inroads of private licentiousness. As to those partial commotions and insurrections which sometimes disquiet society, from the intrigues of an inconsiderable faction, or from sudden or occasional ill humors that do not infect the great body of the community, the general government could command more extensive resources for the suppression of disturbances of that kind than would be in the power of any single member. And as to those mortal feuds, which in certain conjunctures spread a conflagration through a whole nation, or through a very large proportion of it—proceeding either from weighty causes of discontent given by the government, or from the contagion of some violent popular paroxysm—they do not fall within any ordinary rules of calculation. When they happen, they commonly amount to revolutions and dismemberments of empire. No form of government can always either avoid or control them. It is in vain to hope to guard against events too mighty for human foresight or precaution, and it would be idle to object to a government because it could not perform impossibilities. (No. 16)

IF WE mean to be a commercial people, or even to be secure on our Atlantic side, we must endeavor as soon as possible to have a navy. (No. 24)

THE STEADY operations of war against a regular and disciplined army can only be successfully conducted by a force of the same kind. Considerations of economy, not less than of stability and vigor, confirm this position. (No. 25)

War, like most other things, is a science to be acquired and perfected by diligence, by perseverance, by time, and by practice. (No. 25)

Few persons will be so visionary as seriously to contend that military forces ought not to be raised to quell a rebellion, or resist an invasion; and if the defense of the community, under such circumstances, should make it necessary to have an army so numerous as to hazard its liberty, this is one of those calamities for which there is neither preventative nor cure. (No. 26)

The hope of impunity is a strong incitement to sedition—the dread of punishment—a proportionately strong discouragement to it. (No. 27)

[I]f circumstances should at any time oblige the government to form an army of any magnitude, that army can never be formidable to the liberties of the people while there is a large body of citizens little if at all inferior to them in discipline and the use of arms, who stand ready to defend their own rights and those of their fellow citizens. This appears to me the only substitute that can be devised for a standing army; the best possible security against it, if it should exist. (No. 29)

In times of insurrection or invasion it would be natural and proper that the militia of a neighboring state should be marched into another to resist a common enemy, or to guard the republic against the violences of faction or sedition. This was frequently the case in respect to the first object in the course of the late [revolutionary] war; and this mutual succor is indeed a principal end of our political association. If the power of affording it be placed under the direction of the union, there will be no danger of a supine and listless inattention to the dangers of a neighbor, till its near approach had superadded the incitements of self-preservation to the too feeble impulses of duty and sympathy. (No. 29)

It is true, perhaps, that a computation might be made with sufficient accuracy to answer the purpose of the quantity of revenue requisite to discharge the subsisting engagements of the Union, and to maintain those [military] establishments which, for some time to come, would suffice in time of peace. But would it be wise, or would it not rather be the extreme of folly, to stop at this point, and to leave the government intrusted with the care of the national defense in a state of absolute incapacity to provide for the protection of the community against future invasions of the public peace by foreign war or domestic convulsions? If we must be obliged to exceed this point, where can we stop, short of an indefinite power of providing for emergencies as they may arise? Though it is easy to assert, in general terms, the possibility of forming a rational judgment of a due provision against probable dangers; yet we may safely challenge those who make the assertion to bring forward their data, and may affirm that they would be found as vague and uncertain, as any that could be produced to establish the probable duration of the world. Observations confined to the mere prospects of internal attacks can deserve no weight, though even these will admit of no satisfactory calculation. But if we mean to be a commercial people, it must form a part of our policy to be able one day to defend that commerce. The support of a navy, and of naval wars must baffle all the efforts of political arithmetic.

Admitting that we ought to try the novel and absurd experiment in politics of tying up the hands of government from offensive war, founded upon reasons of state, yet certainly we ought not to disable it from guarding the community against the ambition or enmity of other nations. A cloud has been for some time hanging over the European world. If it should break forth into a storm, who can insure us that in its progress a part of its fury would not be spent upon us? (No. 34)

LET US recollect that peace or war will not always be left to our option; that however moderate or unambitious we may be, we cannot count upon the moderation or hope to extinguish the ambition of others. (No. 34)

To JUDGE from the history of mankind, we shall be compelled to conclude that the fiery and destructive passions of war reign in the human breast with much more powerful sway than the mild and beneficent sentiments of peace; and, that to model our political systems upon speculations of lasting tranquility, is to calculate on the weaker springs of the human character. (No. 34)

THERE ARE certain emergencies of nations in which expedients that in the ordinary state of things ought to be foreborn, become essential to the public weal. And the government, from the possibility of such emergencies, ought ever to have the option of making use of them. . . . And as I know nothing to exempt this portion of the globe from the common calamities that have befallen other parts of it, I acknowledge my aversion to every project that is calculated to disarm the government of a single weapon which in any possible contingency might be usefully employed for the general defense and security. (No. 36)

SECURITY against foreign danger is one of the primitive objects of civil society. It is an avowed and essential object of the American Union. The powers requisite for attaining it must be effectually confided to the federal councils. (No. 41)

THE MEANS of security can only be regulated by the means and the danger of attack. They will in fact be ever determined by these rules and by no others. It is vain to oppose constitutional barriers to the impulse of self-preservation. (No. 41)

IT MUST indeed be numbered among the greatest blessings of America, that as her Union will be the only source of her maritime strength, so this will be a principal source of her security against danger from abroad. (No. 41)

IF ONE nation maintains constantly a disciplined army ready for the service of ambition or revenge, it obliges the most pacific nations, who may be within the reach of its enterprises, to take corresponding precautions. (No. 41)

AMONG the advantages of a confederate republic enumerated by Montesquieu, an important one is "that should a popular insurrection happen in one of the States, the others are able to quell it. Should abuses creep into one part, they are reformed by those that remain sound." (No. 43)

BESIDES THE advantage of being armed, which the Americans possess over the people of almost every other nation, the existence of subordinate governments to which the people are attached, and by which the militia officers are appointed, forms a barrier against the enterprises of ambition, more insurmountable than any which a simple government of any form can admit of. (No. 46)

THOSE WHO represent the dignity of their country in the eyes of other nations will be particularly sensible to every prospect of public danger, or of a dishonorable stagnation in public affairs. (No. 58)

IT OUGHT never to be forgotten that a firm Union of this country under an efficient government, will probably be an increasing object of jealousy to more than one nation of Europe. (No. 59)

TO TRACE the mischievous effects of a mutable government would fill a volume. I will hint [at] a few only, each of which will be perceived to be a source of innumerable others.

In the first place, it forfeits the respect and confidence of other nations, and all the advantages connected with national character. An individual who is observed to be inconsistent to his plans, or perhaps to carry on his affairs without any plan at all, is marked at once by all prudent people as a speedy victim to his own unsteadiness and folly. His more friendly neighbors may pity him, but all will decline to connect their fortunes with his, and not a few will seize the opportunity of making their fortunes out of his. One nation is to another what one individual is to another, with this melancholy distinction perhaps: that the former, with fewer of the benevolent emotions than the latter, are under fewer restraints also from taking undue advantage of the indiscretions of each other. Every nation, consequently, whose affairs betray a want of wisdom and stability, may calculate on every loss which can be sustained from the more systematic policy of its wiser neighbors. (No. 62)

WITHOUT A select and stable member of the government [such as a senate], the esteem of foreign powers will not only be forfeited by an unenlightened and variable policy proceeding from the causes already mentioned; but the national councils will not possess that sensibility to the opinion of the world, which is perhaps not less necessary in order to merit, than it is to obtain its respect and confidence.

    An attention to the judgment of other nations is important to every government for two reasons: The one is that, independently of the merits of any particular plan or measure, it is desirable on various accounts that it should appear to other nations as the offspring of a wise and honorable policy. The second is that in doubtful cases, particularly where the national councils may be warped by some strong passion or momentary interest, the presumed or known opinion of the impartial world may be the best guide that can be followed. . . .

    Yet however requisite a sense of national character may be, it is evident that it can never be sufficiently possessed by a numerous and changeable body. It can only be found in a number so small that a sensible degree of the praise and the blame of public measures may be the portion of each individual; or in an assembly so durably invested with public trust that the pride and consequence of its members may be sensibly incorporated with the reputation and prosperity of the community. (No. 63)

THE POWER of making treaties is an important one, especially as it relates to war, peace, and commerce; and it should not be delegated, but in such a mode and with such precautions as will afford the highest security; that it will be exercised by men the best qualified for the purpose, and in the manner most conducive to the public good. (No. 64)

ALTHOUGH THE absolute necessity of system in the conduct of any business is universally known and acknowledged, yet the high importance of it in national affairs has not yet become sufficiently impressed on the public mind. They who wish to commit the power [of ratifying treaties] to a popular assembly composed of members constantly coming and going in quick succession, seem not to recollect that such a body must necessarily be inadequate to the attainment of those great objects which require to be steadily contemplated in all their relations and circumstances, and which can only be approached and achieved by measures which not only talents, but also exact information, and often much time, are necessary to concert and to execute. It was wise therefore in the Convention to provide not only that the power of making treaties should be committed to able and honest men, but also that they should continue in place a sufficient time to become perfectly acquainted with our national concerns, and to form and introduce a system for the management of them. The duration prescribed is such as will give them an opportunity of greatly extending their political informations and of rendering their accumulating experience more and more beneficial to their country. Nor has the Convention discovered less prudence in providing for the frequent elections of senators in such a way [one-third every two years] as to obviate the inconvenience of periodically transferring those great affairs entirely to new men. For by leaving a considerable residue of the old ones in place, uniformity and order, as well as a constant succession of official information, will be preserved.

There are few who will not admit that the affairs of trade and navigation should be regulated by a system cautiously formed and steadily pursued, and that both our treaties and our laws should correspond with, and be made to promote it. It is of much consequence that this correspondence and conformity be carefully maintained; and they who assent to the truth of this position will see and confess that it is well-provided for by making the concurrence of the Senate necessary both to treaties and to laws.

It seldom happens in the negotiation of treaties of whatever nature, but that perfect *secrecy* and immediate *dispatch* are sometimes requisite. There are cases where the most useful intelligence may be obtained if the persons possessing it can be relieved from apprehensions of discovery. Those apprehensions will operate on those persons whether they are actuated by mercenary or friendly motives, and there doubtless are many of both descriptions who would rely on the secrecy of the president, but who would not confide in that of the senate, and still less in that of a large popular assembly. The Convention have done well, therefore, in so disposing of the power of making treaties, that although the president must in forming them act by the advice and consent of the senate, yet he will be able to manage the business of intelligence in such manner as prudence may suggest.

They who have turned their attention to the affairs of men must have perceived that there are tides in them. Tides, very irregular in their duration, strength, and direction, and seldom found to run twice exactly in the same manner or measure. To discern and to profit by these tides in national affairs is the business of those who preside over them; and they who have had much experience on this head inform us that there frequently are occasions when days, nay even when hours are precious. The loss of a battle, the death of a prince, the removal of a minister, or other circumstances intervening to change the present posture and aspect of affairs, may turn the most favorable tide into a course opposite to our wishes. As in the field, so in the cabinet, there are moments to be seized as they pass, and they who preside in either should be left in [a] capacity to improve them. So often and so essentially have we heretofore suffered from secrecy and dispatch, that the Constitution would have been inexcusably defective if no attention had been paid to those objects. Those matters which in negotiations usually require the most secrecy and the most dispatch are those preparatory and auxiliary measures which are not otherwise important in a national view, than as they tend to facilitate the attainment of the objects of the negotiation. For these, the president will find no difficulty to provide, and should any circumstance occur which requires the advice and consent of the Senate, he may at any time convene them. Thus we see that the Constitution provides that our negotiations for treaties shall have every advantage which can be derived from talents, information, integrity, and deliberative investigations on the one hand, and from secrecy and dispatch on the other. (No. 64)

THEY WHO make laws may without doubt amend or repeal them; and it will not be disputed that they who make treaties may alter or cancel them. But still let us not forget that treaties are made not by only one of the contracting parties, but by both, and consequently, that as the consent of both was essential to their formation at first, so must it ever afterwards be to alter or cancel them. The proposed Constitution, therefore, has not in the least extended the obligation of treaties. They are just as binding, and just as far beyond the lawful reach of the legislative acts now, as they will be at any future period or under any form of government. (No. 64)

THE HISTORY of human conduct does not warrant that exalted opinion of human virtue which would make it wise in a nation to commit interests of so delicate and momentous a kind as those which concern its intercourse with the rest of the world, to the sole disposal of a magistrate, created and circumstanced as would be a president of the United States. (No. 75)

THE FLUCTUATING and, taking its future increase into the account, the multitudinous composition of that body [House of Representatives], forbid us to expect in it those qualities which are essential to the proper execution of such a trust [treaty-making]. Accurate and comprehensive knowledge of foreign politics; a steady and systematic adherence to the same views; a nice and uniform sensibility to national character, decision, *secrecy* and dispatch, are incompatible with the genius of a body so variable and so numerous. The very complication of the business, by introducing a necessity of the concurrence of so many different bodies, would of itself afford a solid objection. (No. 75)

# Index

Achean League, 88
Adair, Douglas, 20, 46n
Adams, John, 140
Agriculture, 157, 160. *See also* Farmers
Amendments to Constitution: procedure for, 8, 76, 82, 91; those needed will be adopted, 82
Annapolis Convention, 4, 13
Antifederalists, 6, 51, 53, 56–57, 58, 60, 61, 66, 80, 85, 107, 109–10; in New York, 7, 8; in Virginia, 16
Appointment power, 97–98, 104–5, 138–40, 141; removal power, 140
Arendt, Hannah, 41n
Arms, right to bear, 169, 171
Army, 166–71; Continental, 3, 155; irregulars, 164, 166. *See also* Military establishment; Militia; Navy
Articles of Confederation, 1, 2, 4, 5, 11, 14, 19, 32, 33–34, 35, 42n, 57–58, 91, 131; weakness of, 3, 4, 10–11, 17, 45n, 51–52, 55, 61–62, 62, 70, 75, 88, 155; ratification of, 12, 88; and other confederations, 13, 72, 109; creation of, 55; as foundation for Constitution, 75. *See also* Congress, Continental (Confederation)

Athens, 39, 47n, 123, 128–29. *See also* Greece
Attainder, bills of, 77, 144

Bacon, Francis, 40
Beard, Charles A., 42n
Bicameralism, 39, 99, 108, 127–29. *See also* Checks and balances; Legislature(s)
Bill of rights, 8, 16, 24, 51–52, 66
Bolingbrook, Viscount, 31

Checks and balances, 15, 35, 37–39, 95–96, 127, 128, 139, 143, 147. *See also* Bicameralism; Executive (presidency), veto; Separation of powers
Clinton, George, 6, 7, 7–8
Commager, Henry Steele, 41n–42n, 42n
Commerce (trade): and conflict, 13, 56, 92, 122, 156–58, 163–65, 166–67, 170
Confederacies, 13, 54, 55, 72, 83–88, 109
Congress, Continental (Confederation), 9, 10, 11, 12, 14, 17–18, 19,

# THE EDITOR

QUENTIN P. TAYLOR is author of *The Other Machiavelli: Republican Writings by the Author of "The Prince"* and *The Republic of Genius: A Reconstruction of Nietzsche's Early Thought.* He holds a Ph.D. in Political Science and a M.Ed. in U.S. History from the University of Missouri–Columbia.

# THE CENTER FOR THE STUDY OF THE AMERICAN CONSTITUTION

The foremost institution of its kind, the Center maintains the most extensive archives anywhere of documents related to the drafting and ratification of the U.S. Constitution and the Bill of Rights.

Located at the University of Wisconsin–Madison, the Center hosts research scholars from around the world, conducts it own research, and offers courses, special lectures, and consulting services.

Its publications include *The Documentary History of the Ratification of the Constitution* (21 vols.), *The Documentary History of the First Federal Elections* (4 vols.), *The Constititonal Heritage Series,* and a wide range of monographs.

The Center is under the directorship of Dr. John P. Kaminski and Dr. Richard Leffler.

Designed by William Kasdorf
for Madison House

Typeset in Janson